T4-AKM-573

CONNOISSEURS AND MEDIEVAL MINIATURES

Auguste de Châtillon: Léopoldine au Livre d'Heures, 1835. (*See p.* 143)
Maison de Victor Hugo, Paris: photograph by Bulloz

CONNOISSEURS
AND
MEDIEVAL
MINIATURES
1750–1850

A. N. L. MUNBY

OXFORD
AT THE CLARENDON PRESS
1972

Oxford University Press, Ely House, London W. 1

GLASGOW NEW YORK TORONTO MELBOURNE WELLINGTON
CAPE TOWN IBADAN NAIROBI DAR ES SALAAM LUSAKA ADDIS ABABA
DELHI BOMBAY CALCUTTA MADRAS KARACHI LAHORE DACCA
KUALA LUMPUR SINGAPORE HONG KONG TOKYO

PRINTED IN GREAT BRITAIN
AT THE UNIVERSITY PRESS, OXFORD
BY VIVIAN RIDLER
PRINTER TO THE UNIVERSITY

Preface

THE subject of this book impinges on art history; and art historians, Mr. John Sparrow has recently reminded us, swim in waters inhabited by carnivores. What Siren-song beguiled a historian of libraries to risk his coracle beyond the bar which divides the shark-infested main from lagoons of bibliography and palaeography? Fifteen years' work on the papers of Sir Thomas Phillipps brought me into contact with many other contemporary collectors of books and manuscripts, some of whose papers, in their turn, I sought out. Notes accumulated, and certain patterns of connoisseurship and a few especially influential personalities became discernible. One minor trend and its group of collectors I detached and studied separately in a book published in 1962, *The Cult of the Autograph Letter in England*. There remained a long-held ambition to write in some detail on the men who collected illuminated manuscripts of the middle ages during the century of transition from the classical to the Gothic taste.

A series of Lyell Lectures delivered at Oxford in 1963 dealt with three such collectors, Lord Ashburnham, Walter Sneyd, and Robert Curzon; and the Sandars Lectures at Cambridge in 1970 provided a general survey of the period 1750 to 1850, together with a more detailed study of a particularly significant collector, Francis Douce. These lectures have been recast and expanded: and a preliminary chapter has been added, by kind permission of the editor of *The Times Literary Supplement*, in which it was originally published on 18 April 1968. I have followed the formula evolved in previous books, and decided to treat a handful of collectors at greater length, and, where unpublished papers are available, to investigate their lives as well as their collections. Others may feel as I do that persons are as interesting as objects.

There are many to whom I am indebted. I have benefited from discussing the scheme of this book with Professor Julian Brown, Mr. John Carter, Mr. Anthony Hobson, Mr. N. R. Ker, Sir Roger Mynors, Mr. John Sparrow, and Professor Francis Wormald, and profited from their suggestions. Professor Francis Haskell, who kindly read several chapters in draft, has saved me from a number of art-historical errors and naïvetés, and must on no account be held responsible for those which remain.

My thanks are due to Miss Janet Backhouse of the Department of Manuscripts at the British Museum for sharing with me her deep knowledge of the late schools of illumination which were fashionable during most of the period of which I write. At the Bodleian I have had much help from Dr. R. W. Hunt, Mr. J. J. G. Alexander, and Miss A. C. de la Mare; and at Keele University from the Librarian, Mr. S. O. Stewart, and from the Archivist, Mr. Ian H. C. Fraser. In the United States I found much to my purpose at the Pierpont Morgan Library, New York, and am especially grateful to Mr. John H. Plummer, and to Mr. Frederick B. Adams, Jr., Director at the time of my visit in 1968, when I was indebted to the Morgan Library for a research grant. At the Grolier Club, New York, I am grateful for assistance from the then Librarian, Mr. Gabriel Austin; at Harvard from Mr. William H. Bond; at Yale from Mr. Herman W. Liebert; and at the Henry E. Huntington Library, San Marino, from Mr. James Thorpe. For aid on specific points I gratefully acknowledge the help of Lord Clark, Mr. E. F. Croft-Murray, Dr. A. I. Doyle, Miss Phyllis Giles, Dr. R. J. Hayes, Miss Dorothy Miner, Mr. J. C. T. Oates, Mr. T. C. Skeat, Miss Dorothy Stroud, Dr. C. E. Wright, and others whose assistance is recorded at the appropriate points in the text and footnotes.

To my Cambridge College I am grateful for leave of absence during 1968, and to All Souls College, Oxford, for electing me to a Visiting Fellowship during that leave, to enable me to study intensively the Douce and Heber papers in the Bodleian. Mr. George Rylands has repeated once again the act of friendship which he first performed for me twenty years ago, and has read my entire typescript with an eye sharply critical of the diffuse, the inelegant, and the slipshod. I am deeply grateful to him.

King's College, Cambridge A. N. L. MUNBY

Contents

List of Plates

Between pp. 86 *and* 87

Permission for reproduction is gratefully acknowledged to the Trustees of the British Museum (Plates 1, 2, 11, and 16), of Sir John Soane's Museum (5), of the National Portrait Gallery (10), and of the Pierpont Morgan Library (8 and 9); to the Curators of the Bodleian Library (3, 6, and 7); to the Librarian of the John Carter Brown Library (4), and of the Houghton Library, Harvard University (12 and 14); and to the Curator of the Maison de Victor Hugo, Paris (frontispiece). Dr. R. Sibson was so kind as to photograph no. 13 for me.

I *Introduction ◆ the scope of the investigation stated ◆ a case-history which epitomizes the subject ◆ the vicissitudes of the Bedford 'Missal' during the eighteenth and early nineteenth centuries*

MY subject is the growth of appreciation of the medieval miniature as a work of art, and my period roughly the century which began in 1750. This somewhat specialized aspect of the Gothic revival has not, so far as I know, been studied in any great detail before. At the beginning medieval miniatures were in general little regarded, and those palaeographers and antiquaries who did refer to them were apt to dismiss them as rude monkish drawings which reflected the barbarity of their age. None the less, at this early period, when it was exceptional for anyone to discern artistic merit in them, they were not wholly neglected. Iconographers and antiquaries recognized them as a possible source of information on the features of a king or the shape of a thirteenth-century boot. By 1850 the situation was transformed: they were recognized as part of the history of painting, and an important part for the period before panel-paintings survived in any numbers. The art historians had moved in on them, and Dr. Waagen was analysing techniques and discerning schools and influences: and simultaneously with Waagen's matter-of-fact approach we find Ruskin regarding his illuminated missals as fairy cathedrals full of painted windows. Illumination to medieval patterns vied with tatting and Berlin woolwork as a fitting pursuit for young ladies, and cheap methods of reproduction in colour, such as chromolithography, made illuminated manuscripts familiar to a much wider public.

My aim is to sketch the development of this revolution in taste—to trace appreciation of miniatures from 'Gothic into art'. My inquiry must of necessity be rather diffuse in its range. It will embrace art history, palaeography, and connoisseurship: it will survey the sources of supply, and the market not only in complete manuscripts but also in single miniatures from dismembered manuscripts, which was a common and not wholly agreeable feature of our period. I shall be concerned with collectors, and to some degree with social history, in so far as I shall record how *nouveaux riches* bankers and members of the professional classes became active in what had been largely a patrician field of operation. The personalities and libraries of two or three collectors who, in my view, typify in succeeding generations the changing attitudes, will be studied in depth. And I shall consider in some detail the case-histories of two or three important illuminated manuscripts which conveniently changed hands several times during the century, and thus attracted comment from dealers and collectors and presented tangible evidence of the varying esteem in which they were held—the amount of hard cash which at different points within my period the same item realized in the open market.

It happens that one famous early-fifteenth-century manuscript of the very first rank changed hands no less than seven times within the period under consideration. From the first half of the eighteenth century onwards it was an object of curiosity and admiration, and scholars of succeeding generations—Vertue, Gough, Douce, Dibdin, Madden, and Waagen—recorded their reactions to it, in which can be traced awakening awareness of the artistic value of miniature painting of the late middle ages. So well does this case-history epitomize the subject of this book that it seemed appropriate to recount it by way of introduction, and thus to set the stage for the more extended investigation which will follow.

The manuscript in question, now British Museum Add. MS. 18850, is the Book of Hours, executed between 1423 and 1430 for John, Duke of Bedford, Regent of France, and his first wife, Anne, daughter of John, Duke of Burgundy. So famous a monument of French Gothic art is too well known to merit detailed description here. The profusion and quality of its decoration, and in particular the consummate skill with which miniature portraits of the Duke and Duchess are executed, have earned it a prominent place in all histories of the medieval book; and its ability to bear comparison with any manuscript of the period is unchallenged.

Given in 1430 to the young Henry VI, and later, under circumstances still obscure, in the possession of Henri II and his queen,

Catherine de Medicis, it was in England by the seventeenth century and in the early eighteenth century it was bought from Frances, wife of Sir Robert Worsley, Bt., of Appuldurcombe, by Edward Harley, 2nd Earl of Oxford. The date of acquisition is uncertain and the *Diary* (ed. Wright) of Humfrey Wanley, the Earl's librarian, makes no mention of the transaction: but at this time it was bound in crimson velvet with gold clasps, engraved with the Harley, Cavendish, and Holles arms. By 1743 George Vertue had seen it, for he copied and engraved the portrait of the Duke of Bedford (Plate 1) to illustrate the third edition of Rapin's *History of England*, 'from a curious Limning in a (MS.) rich Prayerbook . . . now in the possession of the Earl of Oxford'.

Vertue's *Note Books* contain a good many references to medieval manuscripts. His main interest was, of course, portraiture, and his notes are largely iconographical. Where he introduces critical comment on script and illumination his greatest enthusiasm is, predictably, directed towards the sixteenth century, especially to the work of Petruccio Ubaldini and Giulio Clovio, who for another three generations were to represent the summit of the illuminator's art. Nevertheless, among earlier manuscripts he diligently sought out portraits of Lydgate and Hoccleve, and found much to admire in the Lovel Lectionary[1] besides the portraits of John, Lord Lovel, and Frater Johannes Siferwas. 'Many other limnings in the book,' he noted, 'finely done of the best stile I have yet seen of that *Age*. Quere if that be the Kings picture in the seat of Judgement.'

Vertue left no record of the occasion on which he first copied the Duke of Bedford's portrait. He made a note, however, when the Bedford Book of Hours changed hands for the first time after the Earl of Oxford's death in 1741, as an incomplete entry of September 1749 in the *Note Books* testifies:

> Lately the Duke & Duchess of Portland being at Welbeck with the Countess Dowager of Oxford her Ladyship presented to her Grace—the most rare book containing the limnings of the famous Julio Clovio which was formerly in the Collection of the Earl of Oxford—now at Bolstrode—and also a most curious prayer book originally the Regent of France the

[1] British Museum, Harl. MS. 7026.

Duke of Bedfords—with his portrait kneeling and also the Duchess—another finely Illuminated book—of the . . .[1]

This is the reason that the Bedford Book of Hours did not pass to the nation when the Harleian manuscripts were acquired for the embryo British Museum in 1753, but for a further century underwent the vicissitudes of the auction room. It first appeared in the *Catalogue of the Portland Museum*, sold by Skinner and Co. in April and May 1786, among the shells, corals, petrifactions, curious agates, dried vegetables, insects, Chinese and Indian artificial curiosities, prints, drawings, miniatures, jewels, the Portland Vase, Queen Elizabeth's buttons, and other objects which comprised the 4,156 lots in the sale of that famous *Kuriositätenkabinett*. The Bedford 'Missal', to give it the misnomer by which it was known for eighty years, was lot 2,951, and although briefly described, attracted strong competition, being secured by the bookseller James Edwards for £213. 3*s*. 0*d*., 'His Majesty declining the competition'.[2] An interesting sidelight on the sale is supplied in a note by Thomas Kirgate, Horace Walpole's printer, in Walpole's copy of Gough's *Account* of the manuscript in the library of Mr. W. S. Lewis at Farmington, Connecticut.

George 3d. meant to purchase this Missal at the Auction of the Duchess of Portland

Kirgate recorded,

and make a present of it to the College of Eton, as having belonged to the Founder of that Seminary Henry 6th and gave unlimited Commission to the learned Jacob Bryant to bid for it—but Mr Bryant hearing above 200£ bidden for it, thought the price too extravagant, and let it go to Mr Edwards the Bookseller, of whom the King would have repurchased it, but Mr Edwards chose to keep it for himself.[3]

The price, a very high one for such a manuscript in an English sale, was not extravagant when compared with the 5,000 livres which was

[1] Walpole Society, xxx (*Vertue Note Books*, vi), 1955, p. 150.

[2] James Dallaway, *Anecdotes of the Arts in England*, 1800, p. 425.

[3] Miss Eleanour P. Spencer has kindly pointed out to me that this note was printed in *The Gentleman's Magazine*, xxxvii (Apr. 1852), p. 322.

inclusion of this manuscript in the *Decameron*, and the superlatives he lavished upon it, gave it an additional cachet in the eyes of contemporary connoisseurs.

The Duke of Marlborough (as the Marquess of Blandford became two years after his purchase) enjoyed possession of the manuscript for little more than a decade. Spendthrift expenditure, which taxed even a ducal income, led to the dispersal of nearly all his great library in his lifetime; and in his declining years at Blenheim 'he lived in utter retirement at one corner of his magnificent palace, a melancholy instance of the results of extravagance'. By 1828 the Bedford 'Missal' was in the hands of John Milner, of 34 York St., Portman Square, an unredeemed pledge for a loan which different sources record as being of £500 and £800. Here it was seen by young Frederic Madden, at the outset of his career in the British Museum Department of Manuscripts, who on June 28, in the company of William Young Ottley, visited Milner's house and recorded his comments: 'It is certainly, and without exception, the most magnificent Ms. I have ever beheld, & highly interesting for the portraits it contains. . . . I covet this Ms. for the Museum exceedingly.'[1] On 20 May 1833 Madden again inspected the manuscript, in the company of Sir Thomas Phillipps, for he had heard that its sale by auction was imminent, and it was duly included in a sale held by Evans beginning on 19 June. Milner's name did not appear, and the Bedford 'Missal', lot 613, was part of an anonymous property attached to the second portion of the library of John Broadley, F.S.A. In general, times were not propitious for the sale, and the slump described in Dibdin's *Bibliophobia*, 1832, had caused prices to decline. Strong competition for the 'Missal', however, between Sir John Soane,[2] William Esdaile,[3] and Sir John Tobin, caused the last-named to pay £1,100 for the lot.

[1] Bodl. MS. Eng. hist. c. 147, f. 120^v.

[2] Soane possessed an important group of manuscripts, of which the most notable was Cardinal Marino Grimani's Commentary on St. Paul's Epistle to the Romans, with miniatures by Clovio.

[3] William Esdaile (1758–1837), banker and print collector. His library, prints, pictures, and *objets* were sold by Christie in eight sales in 1838 and 1840. He owned the famous Missal illuminated by Francesco de Castello, which was subsequentl) damaged in Jarman's flood, now Pierpont Morgan Library MS. 306.

Sir John Tobin, a Liverpool merchant knighted in 1821, when he was Lord Mayor of that city, is an interesting collector. He owned only about seven manuscripts, but their quality was high, and three were of the first rank. On his way back from Ireland on 28 August 1835 Madden called on him at his office in Liverpool and received a cordial invitation to visit his home at Oak Hill, three and a half miles outside Liverpool, on the following day:[1] '29 August 1835. Ordered a car to take me to Sir John Tobin's at ½ past 5 and arrived shortly after six o'clock. Sir John received me, as before, most kindly, and introduced me to Lady Tobin, to his daughter (one of 3: the other two are married) and to his son-in-law Mr. Littledale. The "Missals" were forthwith produced, and are in number 5.' Madden listed on this occasion the Bedford 'Missal'; the Isabel Breviary,[2] bought for £520 at Philip Hurd's sale in 1832; the Book of Hours written for Francis I,[3] with late miniatures added, for which Tobin had given £163. 16*s*. 0*d*. at Sir Mark Masterman Sykes's sale in 1824; the Book of Hours of Juana, daughter of Ferdinand and Isabella, erroneously called the Hours of Mary of Burgundy,[4] from the Hanrott Collection; and the Hours of Francis de Dinteville, Bishop of Auxerre,[5] written in 1525 and acquired by Tobin at the Beckford sale at Fonthill in 1823. 'These are treasures indeed!' commented the professional palaeographer. His host made an equally favourable impression—'not a man of polish or education—but a most generous open-hearted liberal-minded person'. This view of Tobin was shared by Dibdin and, to a higher degree, by G. F. Waagen,[6] who visited Oak Hill in September 1835, and found his host 'a fine man, advanced in years'. Miss Sarah Tobin played hostess, and Waagen noted 'the freedom from constraint which I have before commended in the English ladies, united with much love of art, and a cultured understanding'. Waagen's visit marked the beginning of a new way of looking at the Bedford 'Missal', and indeed at all illuminated manuscripts in this country. For the first time the miniature was seen as part of the history of painting, and

1 Bodl. MS. Eng. hist. c. 150, ff. 225 *et seq.*

2 B.M. Add. MS. 18851.

3 B.M. Add. MS. 18853.

4 B.M. Add. MS. 18852.

5 B.M. Add. MS. 18854.

6 G. F. Waagen, *Works of Art and Artists in England*, iii, 1838, pp. 172–6.

subject to the same critical speculation on schools and ateliers, to the same search for influences and parallels, as were evoked by easel pictures.

Waagen gave a minute account of the manuscript and then passed to judgements. He had no doubt of its quality: 'The splendour with which it is got up, the richness of the pictorial ornaments, renders it one of the most important monuments of this kind, which that age, so fertile in works of art, produced.' He expounded what he considered to be the book's national characteristics, remarking that 'the pictures, as well as the writing and all the ornaments, indicate a Flemish origin'. He calls the Van Eycks to give evidence, 'but the pictures are by no means in the style of Van Eyck when it had attained its perfection, but are rather a transition from the earlier, more conventional, and typical, to the more natural style of the Van Eycks'. He invokes technique: 'In the verdigris colour, and the frequent use of gold, with brown shadows, we recognise the new fashion of the fifteenth century.' He draws comparisons with a similar work and takes issue with a previous critic: 'When Dr. Dibdin affirms in general that this Missal excels in the miniatures the celebrated Breviary of the same Duke of Bedford in the Royal Library of Paris, he has again been carried too far by his patriotic zeal, for the numerous miniatures in the Breviary belong to the free art of Van Eyck in its perfection, and are of such delicacy and beauty as the last three in the Missal . . .'

Until very recently we would have said that on the main issue—Flemish workmanship—Waagen was mistaken, and that the Bedford Book of Hours is one of a well-attested group of French manuscripts. So far as the criticism and appreciation of this book are concerned, we have moved into the modern world. How far we have progressed—but also how distant we are still from any final assessment of the circumstances under which the book was produced, and of the various artists who decorated it—may be judged from Miss Eleanour P. Spencer's learned article in *The Burlington Magazine* in 1965.[1] Moreover, since the publication of that article Miss Spencer has

[1] 'The Master of the Duke of Bedford: The Bedford Hours', *The Burlington Magazine*, cvii (1965), pp. 495–502.

kindly informed me that Waagen's comparison of the miniatures with the art of Van Eyck can be shown to be more perceptive than has hitherto been recognized: and she hopes to publish newly-collected comparative material to demonstrate this point.

By way of epilogue, the acquisition of this splendid manuscript by the British Museum should be recorded. The negotiations, not devoid of excitement, are amply documented in Madden's journals,[1] and the temptation must be resisted to allot them more space than they merit. In 1838 Sir John Tobin gave all his manuscripts to his son, the Revd. John Tobin, of Liscard, Cheshire, and the father died on 27 February 1851. In the course of that year John Boykett Jarman, the well-known dealer in pictures and *objets d'art* of New Bond Street, mentioned to one of the leading booksellers, William Boone, that he would shortly visit Liverpool and proposed to call on Mr. Tobin and ask to see the Bedford 'Missal'. Jarman was himself a dealer in manuscripts, and Boone, fearing that his rival might buy the prize, hurried off to Liverpool first to forestall him. He was successful. When Jarman called, the manuscripts had been sold to Boone, so Tobin assured him, 'at a sacrifice'. Jarman told Madden that he thought the purchase price was not more than £1,500 for seven manuscripts.

On 12 January 1852 Boone called on Madden at the Museum, and, explaining that Lord Ashburnham had declined the group, gave the Trustees next refusal of them for £3,000, a figure Madden thought very large but agreed to submit to his superiors. Madden was anxious to secure them, and much regretted that Tobin had not offered them direct to the National Collection. £2,000 or even £2,500 he felt to be the market value; however, he set to work drawing up a memorandum and getting second opinions from colleagues in the Museum, such as Carpenter of the Print Room and Holmes of Madden's own Department of Manuscripts. On 31 January Madden was summoned to a meeting of the Trustees. 'There were present, the Bp. of London, Lord Cadogan, Sir Robert Inglis, Sir David Dundas, Rt. Hon. H. Goulburn, Lord Mahon, Hamilton, Macaulay and Hallam. The question of purchasing Mr. Boone's

1 Bodl. MS. Eng. hist. c. 165, ff. 16 *et seq.*

Mss. was discussed, on which, to my great surprize, they were all unanimous, *that they were at all events to be secured for the Museum.*' Madden first offered Boone £2,500 for all seven or £2,000 for the best three, a suggestion that the bookseller 'at once and without hesitation *declined*'. Poor Madden was consumed with vexation. 'I could not get the affair out of my mind, and it kept me awake half the night', he recorded.

On 2 February 1852 Boone brought an official reply to the Trustees, stating that he 'could not recede from the sum of Three Thousand Pounds', or divide up the collection, but in conversation with Madden he said that if the Trustees would give £2,500 for the three best he might open negotiations again with Lord Ashburnham for the rest. At this suggestion of once more involving a powerful rival Madden took fright and conceded the bookseller his full price in a letter sent the same day. 'I did not choose to say a word as to the mode of payment,' Madden noted in his journal, 'leaving Mr Boone to arrange that with Sir Henry Ellis. I know that Mr B[oone] is to get £1,500 this year, and the remainder next year, with *interest*, if he insists upon it, but I shall think him a great Jew, if he requires it, after so large a sum has been given him for the mss.'

Such were the slightly undignified circumstances under which Additional Manuscripts Nos. 18850–7, a group which contained one masterpiece and two items of the first rank, entered the Nation's custody.[1]

[1] The British Museum's acquisition of Tobin's MSS. was the subject of a note in *The Gentleman's Magazine*, xxxvii (Mar. 1852), p. 273, a reference kindly given me by Miss Eleanour P. Spencer.

II *Attitudes towards medieval miniatures up to the end of the eighteenth century ⬦ the Abbé Rive ⬦ Wanley ⬦ French tastes infect English collectors ⬦ William Hunter ⬦ Horace Walpole ⬦ the cult of Giulio Clovio ⬦ Thomas Astle ⬦ Joseph Strutt ⬦ Rawlinson's facsimiles ⬦ Mores's reproductions from Bodleian Caedmon ⬦ Sir John Fenn ⬦ R. E. Raspe*

THE range of my researches will now be apparent. In this chapter I shall examine in some detail the attitudes which prevailed towards medieval miniatures up to the end of the eighteenth century.

I start my investigation with the works of the Abbé Jean-Joseph Rive (1730–92). He does not indeed come quite at the beginning of our period, and his writings in their original form had no very wide currency. Two considerations, however, made him influential at second hand, particularly on our side of the Channel. The Abbé Rive became custodian of the famous library of the Duc de La Vallière (1708–80), and was instrumental in gathering together the noble series of fifteenth- and sixteenth-century illuminated manuscripts, many of which came to England after the sale of the Duke's library in the seventeen-eighties: and the Abbé's published views on medieval miniatures, although obscurely put out in the prospectus of a work which was never completed, were lifted in their entirety by the palaeographer Thomas Astle, and incorporated in his excellent and popular book *The Origin and Progress of Writing*.

First, however, a few words of biographical information on the Abbé, an interesting, disagreeable, neurotic, quarrelsome man. The son of a goldsmith, he was ordained young, becoming curé of Mollèges, in the diocese of Arles; he was in Paris in 1767 and became the Duc de La Vallière's librarian late in 1768. His undoubted learning was displayed in a number of works, marred by violent and partisan attacks on all other workers in the field. In particular he seldom lost an opportunity to deride the ignorance and charlatanism of booksellers, and his relish for bitter controversy made him many enemies. To his intense chagrin, after the Duc de La Vallière's death, the heir to the library, the Duchesse de Châtillon, did not commission the Abbé Rive to prepare a catalogue of the collection, but instead placed the task in the hands of the bookseller Guillaume de Bure and his young assistant J. B. van Praet; and the Abbé, predictably, took his revenge by pointing out with relentless asperity the errors in their catalogue. In 1786 he had a stroke, but recovered sufficiently to be appointed Librarian of the library bequeathed by the Marquis de Méjanes to the States of Provence. Here most of his time seems to have been spent in an undignified wrangle about his salary and expenses: he died of apoplexy at Marseilles in 1792.

The *Nouvelle Biographie Universelle*[1] describes the list of his works as interminable, adding the *caveat*, however, that many of them were attested only by the Abbé's own word, and that he was 'apt to describe works projected as works accomplished'. The most extensive book he published seems to be the *Chasse aux bibliographes et antiquaires mal advisés*, 2 vols., 1788–9, described in the text as by a pupil of Rive, but certainly by the Abbé himself, and full of violent attacks on De Bure and Van Praet. 'It is possible', says a critic, 'to meet by chance, amidst this confused mass of minutiae and invective some excellent observations and curious details; but it is buying a very small piece of instruction at the cost of too much disgust and boredom.' The works which concern us here are four that relate to his professional career. The first, *Notices historiques & critiques de deux manuscrits de la bibliothèque de M. Le Duc de La Vallière*, 1779, treats of two fifteenth-century romances of chivalry with miniatures, the first *Le Roman d'Artus*, which subsequently passed into the collections of the Duke of Roxburghe and E. V. Utterson, and the second *Le Rommant de Pertenay*, a manuscript which had previously belonged to two French collectors of romances, Guyon de Sardière and Gaignat. In the following year Rive expanded his account of the former manuscript in a work entitled *Eclaircissements historiques et critiques sur l'invention des cartes à jouer*. In 1785 he published

[1] Vol. xli (1862), pp. 339–40.

a specimen of an ambitious work, *Diverses notices calligraphiques et typographiques, pour servir d'essai à la collection alphabétique de notices calligraphiques de mss. de différents siècles*, scheduled to fill twelve or fifteen volumes, but which in fact described a single late-fifteenth-century manuscript, Galeotti Martii Narniensis Liber Excellentium. This prospectus, which does not seem to have attracted the slightest notice, followed another of a similar kind, published in 1782; it provides justification for the space I am giving to the Abbé Rive.

The *Prospectus* of the unpublished 'Essai sur l'art de vérifier l'âge des miniatures', a duodecimo pamphlet of seventy pages, is uncommon, and still less common when the accompanying twenty-six plates in folio format are present. The Abbé begins by stressing the novelty of his proposed work, the history of painting and calligraphy, and sets out his title in detail: it is an essay on the art of verifying the date of miniatures in manuscripts from the fourteenth to the eighteenth century, and of comparing their different styles and degrees of beauty. Twenty-six plates were envisaged, reproducing the grandest manuscripts in Europe in gold and colours; as well as the history of painting they would illustrate the architecture, customs, and dress of their periods, and thus supplement Montfaucon's *Monuments de la monarchie françoise*. Much stress was laid on the high quality of the proposed plates.

Painting, the author pointed out, had been associated with calligraphy for not less than eighteen centuries. Pliny and Cornelius Nepos provide evidence that manuscripts with miniatures were commissioned in Roman times by Varro and Pomponius Atticus. From the fourth and fifth centuries there survived the Cotton Genesis and the Vatican Vergil and Terence: and almost all manuscripts of this early date were already familiar to connoisseurs, since they had been engraved along with depictions of other surviving relics of Antiquity.

At this point the Abbé Rive expounds the view of medieval art almost uniformly held in the eighteenth century, and indeed slow to be dispelled in the early decades of the nineteenth. 'From the fifth to the tenth centuries', he affirmed, 'the miniatures of manuscripts retain some beauty, especially in Greece . . . From the tenth to the middle of the fourteenth they are almost all frightful, and they reflect the barbarity of the centuries in which they were painted.' Rive's series of facsimiles were to start in the late fourteenth century, when the first dawning of Renaissance art could be discerned, and to lead on to the period which the eighteenth century regarded as the culmination and perfection of the miniaturist's art, the productions of Giulio Clovio and his school in the sixteenth century.

The twenty-six plates, Rive claimed, represented a selection made after examining no less than 12,000 miniatures. There would be accompanying text, setting out the characteristics, artistic, linguistic, and so on, of the manuscripts of each period. The crass ignorance and dishonesty displayed by the booksellers in describing manuscripts would be exposed, and proper standards of judgement laid down. The work, three years in preparation, was nearly complete, and subscribers should receive their copies with no long delay. Eighty copies only would be printed, numbered and certified, at 25 Louis for subscribers; after publication the price was to be raised to 40 Louis.

The Abbé goes on to set out his credentials for writing such a book. He points out that the Duc de La Vallière's library was collected by him in the twelve years from 1768 onwards, and gives a brief account of its formation. He makes some interesting remarks on the origin of the word 'miniature' as applied to decoration of a manuscript, a use of the word which he regards as about a century and a half old when he was writing in 1780: and he cites in evidence the ecclesiastical historian Leone Allacci, who, in his book *De libris et rebus ecclesiasticis Graecorum*, published in 1646, asserts in a passage on the physical attributes of Menologia: 'Picturam recentiores *miniaturam* vocant.' *The New English Dictionary*'s earliest instance of our usage of the word in this sense is by John Evelyn in 1645. Perhaps, however, the most interesting section of Rive's book is his long series of questions, rhetorically posed, which the cataloguer of a manuscript should ask in the course of his work. These seem to me to set a standard of description far higher than was in general use at this date, and indeed to pose a number of problems connected with manuscripts which were hardly recognized by cataloguers for another two or three generations. One cannot summarize the six pages of questions here, but only indicate their scope. Having established the author and the text, says Rive, one must assess the physical attributes of the manuscript in question. Is it in the author's hand, or a copy? If the latter, by whom, where written, and at what date? On what material? With what instrument did the scribe write? In what script? Is the scribe known as the writer of other manuscripts? Are there corrections? Do they derive from the author? What is the provenance of the manuscript? Does it carry armorial bearings or other marks of identification? Has the manuscript been printed? If so, does the manuscript precede publication? Is the text decorated with miniatures? By whom, when, and where, were they executed, and in what style, with what pigments? Are they important in illustrating the manners and customs of their time? This breathless catalogue of shrewd and pertinent queries makes us wish that the Abbé had devoted less of his life to controversy and more to the actual description of manuscripts. Nevertheless, he has claims to our attention as a pioneer in two respects, the technique of cataloguing and the awareness that accounts of medieval miniatures were part of the main stream of the history of painting.

In the British Museum (Add. MS. 15501) is a copy of the Abbé Rive's twenty-six plates, coloured and heightened with gold, and sumptuously bound in red morocco. Descriptions of the plates are added in manuscript, probably by the Abbé himself. Miss Janet Backhouse has pointed out from internal evidence that these descriptions were added after the dispersal of the La Vallière library in 1783 and before 1791.[1] The first plate is of a late-fourteenth-century manuscript, and the last of a seventeenth-century miniature (Plate 2): nos. 22–5 illustrate sixteenth-century books, and all the rest depict miniatures from the grandest and most fashionable manuscripts of the fifteenth century. Having introduced the Abbé Rive at some length, I wish to revert to his dictum that manuscripts with miniatures up to the tenth century were worthy of notice, but that thereafter, until the middle of the fourteenth century, they were not objects with which any Man of Taste should concern himself. I have searched fairly diligently for literature on book-paintings, but precious little is to be found before about 1780. Christian Gottlieb

[1] *British Museum Quarterly*, xxxi, Number 3–4, p. 95, n. 10.

Schwarzius published between 1707 and 1711 three disputations at Altdorf, *De ornamentis librorum apud veteres*, and he presided at a further disputation at Altdorf in 1733, *De ornamentis codicum veterum*, by Philippus Ludovicus Huth, one presumes a pupil of Schwarzius. Palaeographical writers from Montfaucon to Astle are hardly concerned with illumination and miniatures at all, except where the decipherment of intricately decorated capital letters was concerned. In his *Iter Italicum* Montfaucon dismisses the Vatican Vergil in a few lines, describing it as 'of very great Antiquity, in the uncial Character, with Figures in Miniature, by an unskilful Hand'.[1] His only additional comment on the miniatures notes that the horsemen in them had no stirrups. Thanks to Dr. and Mrs. Wright's immaculately indexed edition of Humfrey Wanley's *Diary*,[2] the reactions of Lord Oxford and his librarian to certain fine manuscripts are readily at hand. Wanley's approach to manuscripts was textual and there are very few references to illumination or miniature-painting. His preoccupations were Greek manuscripts and Latin examples of high antiquity, exemplifying the Abbé Rive's first generalization. We see Wanley in the *Diary* failing to acquire for his master the Duke of Devonshire's Benedictional of St. Æthelwold and the Dean and Chapter of Lichfield's St. Chad's Gospels, and succeeding in buying at auction in Holland the famous *Codex Aureus*; in his description of the last the four miniatures of the Evangelists are recorded, but they merit no epithet. References to individual later manuscripts are few, but one is not insignificant. On 21 June 1721 Lord Oxford was shown by Wanley the Lovel Lectionary, but declined to purchase it, 'the whole being but a fragment, & the Pictures & Armes belonging to Families not of his Kindred'. There is no indication that the book's importance as one of the few manuscripts with a first-class miniature signed by the artist, John Siferwas, was appreciated. Nevertheless, one must add that when the manuscript appeared in the auction-room twelve years later Harley laid out £3. 11*s*. 0*d*. to acquire it.[3] I am, of course, far from suggesting that Harley had no interest in the acquisition of the finest illuminated manuscripts of the Abbé

[1] English translation (1712), pp. 325–6.

[2] Bibliographical Society, 2 vols., 1966.

[3] B.M. Harl. MS. 7026.

Rive's dark period; to make such an assertion of the owner of, for example, the Guthlac Roll[1] and the Psalter of Philippa of Hainault would be absurd. It is, however, difficult to find evidence that such manuscripts were acquired for their artistic rather than their antiquarian value. Such artistic interest as there was was more obviously expended on the early and very late schools of decoration.

One other French collector of the mid eighteenth century merits our attention, Antoine-René de Voyer d'Argenson, Marquis de Paulmy (1722–87), founder of the Arsenal Library. His own manuscript catalogue of his books[2] contains notes on individual items which show that views so extreme as the Abbé Rive's were not universally held in France, although the general pattern of his connoisseurship is similar. For my knowledge of the Marquis de Paulmy and his notes I am much indebted to Mr. Anthony Hobson, who sent me the transcripts from them which follow. Of an Apocalypse of the eleventh century the Marquis de Paulmy writes that 'les miniatures sont très ridicules et mal faites; preuve de l'antiquité du Mst.', and of a tenth-century Commentary on the Apocalypse his comment is that '[les miniatures] sont du plus mauvais dessein possible, ce qui prouve encore l'antiquité'. He begins to wax enthusiastic in the fourteenth century; the famous Térence des ducs (Arsenal MS. 664), for example, written about 1400, is 'de la plus grande beauté', and there are similar commendations of many of the grand French and Flemish manuscripts of the fourteenth and fifteenth centuries which he owned. He shows proper discrimination over the enormous range of quality to be found in Books of Hours: 'Ce Mss. [*sic*] et les autres du même genre compris dans ce catalogue sont la plus part beaux, et quelquesuns sont curieux; mais en générale les heures Msstes sont les Msstes les plus communs et l'on ne doit rechercher que les plus belles, et les plus singulières.'

Even in the mid eighteenth century, of course, the supply of fine illuminated books of the tenth century and earlier was limited. In France by that date the most fashionable manuscripts were already

[1] The Guthlac Roll was displayed to the embryo Society of Antiquaries at the Young Devill Tavern on 23 Jan. 1708, and on 15 Mar. 1743 Vertue exhibited to the Society his drawings of miniatures from the Cotton Genesis. See Joan Evans, *A History of the Society of Antiquaries*, Oxford, 1956, pp. 37 and 97.

[2] Arsenal MSS. 6279–97.

the sumptuously illustrated volumes written for patrons at the Parisian and Burgundian courts in the late fourteenth and fifteenth centuries, especially romances of chivalry. The dispersal of the libraries of Guyon de Sardière (1759), Louis-Jean Gaignat (1769), and the Duc de La Vallière (1783 and 1788) brought a whole series of magnificent late manuscripts on to the market, and at these sales several British collectors were active, among them William Hunter (1718–83), the anatomist, whose splendid museum survives in its entirety at Glasgow. Three other dispersals of French collections which were sold by auction on this side of the Channel were influential in introducing English collectors to the expensive tastes of the Continent. Two are well known, but the earliest is rather obscure. In August 1775 died the Revd. Caesar De Missy, preacher at the French Chapel at St. James's, of whom there is an interesting memoir in Nichols's *Literary Anecdotes*.[1] The auction of his substantial library was held by Baker and Leigh on 18 March 1776 and the seven following days. He owned some important Greek manuscripts, and the British Museum laid out £30. 10*s*. 0*d*. on lot 1631, an eleventh-century Gospels brought from Mount Athos. De Missy had spent his life gathering materials for an edition of the New Testament, and his collation is preserved with the original (B.M. Add. MS. 4949). Six other Greek gospels and lectionaries were bought by William Hunter, as well as a group of Greek classical and patristic texts. What was unusual in De Missy's sale was a section of seventeen lots (1648–64) headed 'Missals &c.', among the purchasers of which we find the name of Count MacCarthy-Reagh, who became a French subject during this year. This great collector's library is best known from the sale catalogue prepared after his death by De Bure in 1815. On 18 May 1789, however, Leigh and Sotheby began to hold an anonymous sale of 'a very elegant and curious Cabinet of Books lately imported from France . . . together with a considerable number of manuscripts, both on vellum and paper, the greater part of which contain elegant paintings and illuminations'. The Cabinet was MacCarthy's, and the manuscripts included a whole series of splendid fifteenth-century French volumes, three copies, all with miniatures,

[1] Vol. iii (1812), pp. 305–14.

of *La Tierce Decade* of Livy, for example, a similarly grandly decorated Quintus Curtius, an 'Histoire Historiale, full of miniatures', and the Chroniques de St. Denis, 'a very thick volume, exceedingly full of fine paintings in miniature and initials and other ornaments illuminated'. The grandest of these were bought by collectors who bear famous and patrician names—Egerton, Lansdowne, and Grafton. Others passed to an obviously interesting but little-studied connoisseur, John Jackson, F.S.A., and reappeared in their turn at the sale of his library held in 1794 after his death. Many of the earliest manuscripts, however, were bought for small prices by that exceptionally discriminating collector Francis Douce, to whom the next chapter will be devoted. It was Douce who bought 'a very ancient Psalter, with illuminated miniatures in the initials', for 8*s.* 6*d.*, and, more notably, 'La Bible, traduite en François, par Du Moulin, *written in the 13th century, with 156 miniatures in the coarse manner of that age*, 2 vols., folio', for £7 (Plate 3). Both the mode of description and the price denote limited appreciation, and certainly in 1789 this was a somewhat advanced taste.

More typical—in fact the epitome of French connoisseurship of the period—was the *Bibliotheca Parisina*,[1] brought to London for sale in 1791 by the bookseller James Edwards, an influential figure in disseminating an interest in French styles among English collectors, whom we have already met as the owner of the Bedford 'Missal'. The printed books were the choicest copies, on vellum or large paper and clothed in morocco by Derome. The manuscripts were almost without exception of the fifteenth century or later. Lot 145 was a vellum copy of the Abbé Rive's facsimiles, for which Lord Gainsborough paid £56. 14*s.* 0*d.* Romances of chivalry, chronicles, and a few late Books of Hours represented the high-water mark of acquisition by the Man of Taste: and they set a style in the collecting of manuscripts which was to persist throughout the next generation, the group of collectors who looked to the Roxburghe Club and the publications of its secretary, T. F. Dibdin, as their pattern and inspiration. Already in the third quarter of the eighteenth century

[1] For ownership of this collection see Mr. Arthur Rau's article in *The Book Collector*, xviii, No. 3 (Autumn 1969), pp. 307–17.

such books were being assembled by William Hunter. He did, it is true, acquire a few great treasures of an earlier period, notably the twelfth-century York Psalter with thirteen full-page miniatures: but it is probable that he viewed with greater pride books such as his fifteenth-century copy of Jehan Mielot's 'Le Miroir de l'Humaine Salvation', or his Boccaccio, 'De Casibus Virorum et Foeminarum', 1472, both with fine miniatures, and especially his three-volume French text of the *Vita Christi* of Ludolphus de Saxonia, magnificently illustrated, which had fetched 220 livres at the Gaignat sale.

Hunter on this side of the Channel was a fairly early entrant into this French and patrician field of connoisseurship. One is tempted to name another collector of the previous generation, Ralph Palmer, of Little Chelsea. I say 'tempted' because, even with the help of Mr. Neil Ker's notes, I have a list of only a dozen or so manuscripts he owned, bearing the inscription 'Bibliotheca Palmeriana', and some of them the date 1747. Palmer, however, obviously had a fine eye for quality, for his manuscripts included two such superb books as the Hamilton Gospels (Pierpont Morgan Library MS. 23), authoritatively dated by Dr. E. A. Lowe in the tenth century, but placed by previous scholars up to three centuries earlier; and, even more remarkably, Volume II of the Foucquet Josephus, reunited with the first volume in 1906 by Edward VII as a gesture of *entente cordiale*. One would like to know more of the wanderings of that fifteenth-century masterpiece, especially when and how half of it came to England.

How early can we trace appreciation of what we now regard as the finest period of Gothic illumination? Had Horace Walpole, a connoisseur of advanced tastes in many respects, a feeling for it? In fact he was not a notable collector of such things—'I set little store by a collection of Mss.', he wrote to William Cole on 23 July 1782. Nevertheless, in the Tribune at Strawberry Hill he displayed a few manuscripts, and it is instructive to contemplate the two he valued most highly. They were both of the sixteenth century, and in this choice Walpole was entirely in line with the taste of his day. The first was a Missal executed at Rome in 1532, described by Walpole as having 'miniatures by Raphael and his scholars', and in a gold and jewelled Renaissance binding. Dr. Richard Mead, at whose sale in

1755 Walpole bought it for £42, is said to have given £100 for it, and Walpole believed that it was executed for Queen Claude, wife of Francis I of France. The subsequent history of this elegant piece of *bijouterie* is interesting. At the Strawberry Hill sale in 1842 Lord Waldegrave bought it in for £115. 10*s*. 0*d*. After its exhibition at the Victoria and Albert Museum in 1862 it passed into the possession of Alfred de Rothschild, and thence into the hands of the Countess of Carnarvon, at whose sale in 1925 Lord Rothermere bought it for £2,100. It was resold for £2,500 in 1942 to Messrs. S. J. Phillips, of Bond Street. The other manuscript was even more famous, and has been similarly dethroned by changing values in taste. Its early provenance was patrician indeed, for it belonged both to Thomas Howard, Earl of Arundel, and to Edward Harley, Earl of Oxford. George Vertue wrote a description of it in 1748 for the latter's widow:[1]

> A Rare and curious Manuscript in Latin containing the Psalms of David, done on the finest vellum richly adorn'd and bound, with chased corners and clasps of Gold finely wrought. all the Psalmes are writ with the neatest Pen from the beginning to the end. it is adorn'd with the finest illuminations by the Famous Limner & Miniature Painter, DON JULIO CLOVIO. The illuminations of the Figures (6) and the Borders are 21 of the highest perfection, and for the beauty of colours enrichments of ornaments, beyond comparison. This Book was Inscrib'd to the Noble Prince, the Duke of Anjou by Clovio, A° MDXXXVII . . . Clovio principally excell'd in miniature painting, with such admirable skill that neither antient nor Moderns can compare with his works . . .

When this splendid object came on to the market at the Duchess of Portland's sale in 1786, Walpole bought it for £169. 10*s*. 0*d*., and recorded in a note[2] the commendation of another connoisseur, Robert Udny of Teddington, who formed a notable collection of pictures. 'Mr Udny assured Mr W.', the note runs, 'he had seen six more by the same hand, but none of them so fine or so well preserved.' The auctioneer of the contents of Strawberry Hill in 1842

[1] Inserted in the MS., now in the John Carter Brown Library.

[2] In his copy of the Portland sale catalogue, in the library of Mr. W. S. Lewis, Farmington, Connecticut.

lavished his superlatives upon it. 'A truly valuable and matchless volume', he printed in his boldest type, 'pronounced by the Cognoscenti as the most wonderful of the works of art which adorn this rare collection.' Lord Waldegrave bought the volume in for £441. When one recalls that eleven years later the Book of Armagh changed hands for £300, the remarkable alteration in our scale of value can be appreciated. In 1887 F. S. Ellis was offering Lord Waldegrave's manuscript for sale, and commissioned from W. H. J. Weale, the liturgiologist, a pamphlet describing the book.[1] Weale cut his subject down to size, and on the title-page it is described as 'an illuminated Psalter for the use of the convent of Saint Mary of the Virgins at Venice, executed by a Venetian artist of the sixteenth century'; while commending its quality, he casts a cold art-historical eye over its reputed artist and early history. 'The style of the designs and the manner of their execution', he wrote, 'is entirely dissimilar to all the authentic works of Giulio Clovio, to whom it was long attributed. Neither can it have been executed for a Prince of the house of Anjou, an absurd misinterpretation of the inscription on the base of a pillar in the miniature of S. Andrew.' Today this formerly celebrated manuscript (Plate 4), now relegated to being a good example of the illuminator's art at an unfashionably late period, is in the John Carter Brown Library, Providence, Rhode Island.

This is the point at which to say something about the cult of Giulio Clovio, who throughout the eighteenth century and well into the nineteenth represented the topmost pinnacle of the miniaturist's achievement. Our modern eyes, which, temporarily at any rate, have ceased to regard the decoration of manuscripts as a form of easel painting in miniature, find the adulation paid to Clovio almost incomprehensible. There were good reasons for it, apart from the premium which the early connoisseurs set on technique and a high polish. Vasari, the *cognoscente*'s *vade-mecum*, had praised him to the skies for his book decoration, and had drawn attention to a number of authentic and well-documented examples of his work. Jonathan Richardson, in his *An Account of the Statues, Bas-reliefs, Drawings, and Pictures in Italy and France*, 1722, a book of great influence, described

[1] *Psalterium et Cantica*, 8°, 50 copies, privately printed, 1887.

various manuscripts by the master which he had sought out in his travels. His comment at times fell short of total enthusiasm—'most beautiful colouring, but upon a Tinct pretty gaudy and wanting simplicity', he wrote of a manuscript in the Vatican. But at Clovio's best, in the Missal in the Ducal Gallery at Parma, for example, he found everything to admire, especially the 'chaste and gentle taste', with its 'inclination towards the style of M. Angelo, but without his extravagance'. Giulio Clovio was the name which was indiscriminately attached by optimistic cataloguers and connoisseurs to almost any showy book of the sixteenth century, and the sums paid for these pretty objects from the twilight of painted book-decoration were truly astounding. I have been at some pains to ascertain when the earliest piece of book-painting by Clovio, now recognized as authentic, came to England. My present candidate is the Commentary by Cardinal Marino Grimani on St. Paul's Epistle to the Romans, now in Sir John Soane's Museum (Plate 5). This belonged successively to those two perceptive connoisseurs, both British Residents in Venice, Consul Smith and John Strange. The Clovio manuscript was lot 735 in the latter's sale at Sotheby's on 19 March 1801, when it realized £76. 13*s*. 0*d*. In 1833 Soane paid no less than £735 for it, an enormous sum for a representative of a school of painting which younger connoisseurs were already beginning to regard as less than supreme. The other very well-known example of Clovio's work, the Stuart de Rothesay Book of Hours,[1] was a nineteenth-century importation. I have traced no engraved copies of Clovio's book-painting to which eighteenth-century collectors would have had access, and it is hard for us to visualize the difficulties under which connoisseurs laboured before the advent of photography and cheap processes of reproduction. Through taking Vasari's judgement of Clovio's supremacy on trust, and through a natural failure to recognize and differentiate his work from that of his contemporaries, collectors attached extravagant values to all sixteenth-century miniature painting.

In the eighteenth century what comments can we find on illumination of the twelfth to the fourteenth centuries? The palaeographer

[1] B.M. Add. MS. 20927.

Thomas Astle of course looked at a large number of manuscripts of the period, and has some valuable comments on, and facsimiles of, their scripts in his *Origin and Progress of Writing*, 1784, but his treatment of the decoration of books is, to say the least, perfunctory. In his eighth chapter he devotes six pages to 'Paintings, Ornaments and Illuminations', and gives the briefest sketch of the history of the illuminator's art. He cites nine manuscripts ascribed by him to the tenth century or earlier, among them most of the more obvious examples; the Cotton Genesis; the Vatican Vergil; the Gospels of St. Augustine at Corpus Christi College, Cambridge, of St. Cuthbert among the Cottonian manuscripts, and of St. Chad at Lichfield. He also cites another tenth-century Gospels, Harleian MS. 2820, as displaying 'Roman drawings of a singular kind'. The list then gets very odd. Harleian MSS. 432, 1802, and 5280 are cited as 'specimens of the ornamented letters, which are to be found in Irish mss. from the 12th to the 14th century'; of these even No. 1802, the Maelbrigt Gospels, 1138, with its debased Anglo-Hibernian decoration, is a singular inclusion in a list which omits the Book of Kells. A copy of Terence in the Bodleian 'displays the dresses, masks, &c. worn by comedians in the twelfth century, if not earlier': and, as a parallel example of the art of drawing in England of the same period, the 'very elegant Psalter in the Library of Trinity College, Cambridge', is cited.[1] Lambeth MS. 471, a thirteenth-century Vergil, 'written in Italy, shows both by the drawing and writing that the Italians produced works much inferior to ours at that period',[2] while the Lambeth Apocalypse (MS. 209) is said to contain 'a curious example of the manner of painting in the fourteenth century':[3] and Harleian MSS. 1319 and 2278 get typical antiquary's commendation as 'curious specimens of manners and customs, both civil and military, at the close of the fourteenth and in the beginning of the fifteenth century'. Astle then goes on to refer to the Abbé Rive's forthcoming book, and pays him the compliment of translating from the prospectus, without acknowledgement of its source, the Abbé's dismissal

[1] MS. No. 987, the Canterbury Psalter.

[2] M. R. James (*Cat. of Lambeth MSS.*, Pt. iv, 1932, p. 646) says: 'Probably the hand is Italian: but I have doubted whether it might not be English.'

[3] It is of the late XIIIth century.

of Gothic illuminated manuscripts as 'so many monuments of the barbarity of those ages'. 'Towards the latter end of the fourteenth century', Astle concludes, 'the paintings in manuscripts were much improved; and in the two succeeding centuries many excellent performances were produced, especially after the happy period of the restoration of the arts.' Astle's list, with its paucity of examples, its notable omissions, and its barren pieces of commentary, certainly epitomizes the ignorance as well as the taste of the period. In justice it must of course be stressed that the short chapter on the decoration of books was quite incidental to the main purpose of his book, which was palaeographical: and Astle himself formed a notable collection of medieval manuscripts, which passed via the Stowe and Ashburnham libraries into the British Museum. The whole bias of Astle's manuscript-collecting was historical and antiquarian rather than artistic: none the less he acquired incidentally a few notable decorated books, the eleventh-century register, for example, of New Minster and Hyde Abbey, with its important line drawings.[1]

The Englishman who without question minutely examined the most medieval miniatures during this early period was Joseph Strutt (1749–1802), the engraver and antiquary. His *Regal and Ecclesiastical Antiquities of England*, 1773, with its numerous representations of kings, costumes, armour, etc., largely copied from depictions in manuscripts, was the earliest work of its kind published in England; and in his *Compleat View of the Manners, Customs, Arms, Habits, &c. of the Inhabitants of England*, 3 vols., 1774–6, he widened the scope of his researches and reproduced a whole series of miniatures, which brought this form of medieval art for the first time before educated readers. His method was not, indeed, original, as he himself pointed out when he drew attention to *Les Monuments de la monarchie françoise*, by Montfaucon, 5 vols., 1729–33, a work to which that great palaeographer had also brought his uniquely wide observation of manuscript illustrations to elucidate the antiquities of his native land. Strutt's *Dresses and Habits of the English People*, 2 vols., 1796–9, and his oft-reprinted *Sports and Pastimes of the People of England*, 1801,

[1] B.M. Stowe MS. 944: Astle's album of copies of scripts and miniatures, as well as some original leaves and a set of Rive's plates, is Stowe MS. 1061.

reproduced hundreds of miniatures and details from originals in colour, and the source of each is exactly specified. His standing as an antiquary is still high, and art historians might do worse than study a short appendix to the third volume of his *Compleat View*, published in 1776, to which Mr. Michael Hunter first drew my attention. This seven-page essay, 'A short account of the rise and progress of the art of design in England', has, for its date, some interesting features. Strutt reproduces, but cannot commend, the four Evangelist miniatures from the Lindisfarne Gospels. By the time he had reached Matthew Paris, however, his enthusiasm was aroused. His designs, he asserted, 'are so well done that many artists of the present age need not be ashamed to own them'. 'In the reign of Edward the Fourth', Strutt stated a few paragraphs later, 'the MS. delineations are very beautiful, and the designs executed (though still in the Gothic stile) with great accuracy and fidelity', and he singles out for praise Cotton Julius E. IV, the Life of Richard Beauchamp, Earl of Warwick, with its 'pretty, though slight designs' by John Rouse. He also in a later work especially commended Queen Mary's Psalter, of which he engraved twelve plates for a small separate publication of 1792,[1] a manuscript which he describes as 'superb' and 'equal, if not superior, in point of workmanship' to anything he had ever seen of that era.

We can see Strutt at work when we examine a manuscript in the Bodleian Library (MS. Douce e. 18) entitled, by Douce, 'Mr Strutt's account of the Mss. that have illuminations, as they occur in various English libraries (with corrections) and additions by F.D.'. Strutt's interest in miniatures as a key to antiquities is underlined, and we find him judging as 'useless' some fine books which do not throw light on the costume or social life of their day. Strutt's notes are undated, but may have been made in the seventeen-seventies: Douce's additions are perhaps twenty years later, and it is interesting to see the former's rather bald *aide-mémoire* expanded by Douce, with notes which show greater artistic appreciation. Thus, in respect of MS. Royal 19 B. XV Strutt notes that it is 'a very beautiful ms. with many curious drawings relative to ancient habits', whereas Douce adds that

[1] See p. 6 above.

'the drawings are, as to outline, in pen and ink and slightly tinted with colour. Many are exceedingly beautiful as to design. The horses too are well drawn. They are the performance of a superior artist. See f. 10 where 2 angels receive some kneeling figures &c. One is reminded of the Cupid and Psyche gem.'[1]

Strutt's works, and those of other contemporary antiquaries, such as Francis Grose and John Brand, acclimatized the reader's eye to the Gothic miniature. Facsimiles had indeed been produced before in small editions for special purposes, notably by Richard Rawlinson (1690–1755), many of whose original copper plates passed with his collections to the Bodleian Library. In particular he was interested in distributing reproductions of some of his early charters; and he exhibited and circulated prints of them at meetings of the Society of Antiquaries. When family misfortunes compelled him to disperse in ten sales the splendid library of his brother Thomas, he had engravings made before the sale of 'some specimens of several hands of the most antient, fair and best mss.'. To this group belong his facsimiles of folio 2 of the tenth-century Arator,[2] and the reproduction of the miniature of an Evangelist in a tenth/eleventh-century copy of the Gospels at St. John's College, Oxford,[3] which he had engraved in 1754.[4] Also noteworthy is the series of facsimiles of miniatures which in 1754 Edward Rowe Mores produced in a small edition from the Anglo-Saxon Cædmon in the Bodleian.[5] The fifteen plates, with title-page and a leaf of Latin Introduction by Mores, are, I believe, the earliest substantial facsimile of an English manuscript.[6] They belong to the revival of Saxon scholarship rather than to the field which we are considering; their purpose was purely antiquarian, as

[1] The most famous antique intaglio in the Marlborough collection; see *Gemmarum Antiquarum Delectus . . . in dactyliothecis Ducis Marlburiensis*, i, 1781, Pl. L.

[2] Bodl. MS. Rawl. c. 570.

[3] MS. 194.

[4] For Rawlinson's facsimiles see Mr. B. J. Enright's unpublished thesis, 'Richard Rawlinson, collector, antiquary and topographer', 1956 (Bodl. MS. D.Phil. d. 1786), pp. 301–3. I am grateful for Mr. Enright's kind permission to consult this.

[5] MS. Junius 11.

[6] See Edward Rowe Mores, *A Dissertation upon English Typographical Founders and Founderies* (1778), ed. Harry Carter and Christopher Ricks, Oxford, 1961, pp. xxi–xxiv. A small second edition of these Cædmon illustrations was made from the same plates about 1830.

the Latin title-page makes clear, when it describes the pictures as designed to illustrate the manners, customs, and buildings of the Anglo-Saxons of the tenth century.

Another antiquary with an eye for a miniature was Sir John Fenn, the first editor of the Paston Letters. In the British Museum is a transcript made for Dawson Turner of an interesting catalogue by Fenn of the collection of manuscripts belonging to one of his Norfolk neighbours—

A descriptive catalogue of the curious and truly valuable manuscripts of Brigg Price Fountaine Esquire of Narford in Norfolk comprehending a most rare collection of illuminated Breviaries,—Psalters—Ordinals—Bibles & Treatises on Ancient Customs, Arts & Sciences; including likewise some ancient & curious Printed Breviaries, Prayer-Books, &c., collected by that great antiquary Sir Andrew Fountaine, Knight, in various parts of Europe.[1]

Fenn's Preface is dated from East Dereham, 10 February 1777. He sets himself high standards of description. 'I have endeavoured', he notes, 'where I had any certain Guide, to ascertain their age, their country, & by whom written and illuminated', but, as was natural enough at that date, ambition outstripped performance. The merits of Fenn's catalogue are to be found in his conscientious attempts to describe the subject of each miniature, in his identification of armorial bearings, his interest in medieval provenances, and his careful pen-facsimiles of fifteenth-century inscriptions of ownership: and at a date when almost all service-books were apt to be lumped together as 'missals', it is refreshing to find a liturgical section in the Preface differentiating Breviaries, Psalters, Ordinals, and Rituals.[2]

Fenn has another claim to our notice, as an early owner of miniatures cut from a manuscript, a practice which will occupy us at some length in a later chapter. Pierpont Morgan Library MS. 126 is a noble folio text of Gower's *Confessio Amantis*, written in the second half

[1] B.M. Add. MS. 22931.

[2] Corrected by Dawson Turner in 1846, at the behest of Dr. F. C. Husenbeth (1796–1872), the Roman Catholic liturgiologist and hagiographer, who himself commissioned illuminated service books.

of the fifteenth century and decorated with 108 miniatures of high quality. It had belonged successively to two great eighteenth-century antiquaries who had collected manuscripts to further their researches, Peter le Neve (1661–1729), Norroy King of Arms, and Thomas Martin, of Palgrave (1697–1771).[1] At Martin's death in 1771 the manuscript of Gower was bought by Thomas Worth, a chemist of Diss in Norfolk, who cut out nine of the miniatures and sold them to Sir John Fenn, whereas the manuscript itself with its remaining 99 miniatures was purchased by Brigg Price Fountaine of Narford. John Pierpont Morgan bought the book from Quaritch after the Fountaine sale in 1902, and by a rare stroke of fortune was able to acquire and reinsert the missing miniatures which came on to the market in 1926 at the sale of the library of Fenn's great-nephew. One would like to know more of Fenn's purpose in being a party to the mutilation. Perhaps in those more casual days it was his purpose to have the extracted miniatures copied and engraved for some antiquarian work; but if he did so, I have not been successful in tracing it.[2]

I have already remarked upon the comparatively little information which is to be found in print before 1800 on medieval miniatures. It is true that many finely decorated manuscripts passed through the auction-rooms, but their descriptions were often quite notably uninformative. 'Heures, or Hours, a Catholick Book of Prayer, *most magnificently illum. and bound in morocco*', is a typical entry. Walpole's *Anecdotes of Painting*, based on Vertue's notebooks, has a very few references in Chapter II of the first volume (1762), and those mainly iconographical. In 1800, when James Dallaway published his supplementary *Anecdotes of the Arts in England*, half a dozen manuscripts are commended for their illumination, including the Sherborne Missal, which, however, Dallaway misdates as early as 1339. A more

[1] Both Martin and his young protégé, John Ives (1751–76), the Yarmouth antiquary, owned among their collections a few finely illuminated volumes of the Gothic period, but there is little evidence to show that their reasons for possessing them were other than purely antiquarian.

[2] Other cuttings from manuscripts owned by Fenn are lots 865–72, 926, and 927 in *Catalogue of the Extraordinary Collection of Autographs, Historical MSS., Deeds, Charters, &c. formed by Sir John Fenn*, sold by Puttick & Simpson, 16–18 July 1866.

fully considered list of ten manuscripts pre-eminent for their decorative qualities was added by Dallaway to his new edition of Walpole's *Anecdotes*, published in 1828, including the Lutterell Psalter and the Life of Richard Beauchamp, Earl of Warwick. Walpole, however, was keenly interested in the origin of painting in oils, and we will end this chapter with a reference, which owes much to the kindness of Mr. J. C. T. Oates, to a book on the techniques of medieval painting, the publication of which he financed in 1781, R. E. Raspe's *A critical essay on oil-painting; proving that the art of painting in oil was known before the pretended discovery of John and Hubert Van Eyck; to which are added, Theophilus de arte pingendi, Eraclius de artibus Romanorum. And a review of Farinator's Lumen Animae.*

Raspe, the future author of Baron Munchhausen's *Travels*, whose thefts from the Landgrave of Hesse's museum of antique gems and medals had led to his flight to England, arrived in Cambridge in 1779, having assumed the rank of Major for his visit. Armed with scalpels, lavender-water, and other concoctions, he presented himself at the University Library, where the obliging Librarian, Dr. Farmer, allowed him to conduct certain tests on a painted mummy-case, but denied him unrestricted access to MS. Ee. 6. 39, a thirteenth-century text of Theophilus, *De diversis artibus*. Mr. Oates has pointed out to me that the initial letter on the first leaf has a smeared and washed-out appearance, but it must be mere surmise whether Farmer caught the reader testing the nature of the illuminator's pigments. It is indeed more likely that Raspe's reputation as a thief had preceded him. Farmer's alleged discourtesy earned him a furious rebuke in Raspe's Preface, where librarians are described as impotent or jealous 'literary eunuchs'.[1] At Trinity College, however, Raspe found not only another text of Theophilus but also a more compliant librarian. Against this rather odd background Raspe's Theophilus, which has been called the 'encyclopaedia of Christian art', describing in great detail most of the medieval skills and crafts, illumination included, was given to the world. Raspe must not be accorded priority as the

[1] A reference to a couplet in Edward Young's *Love of Fame*:

> Unlearned men of books assume the care
> As Eunuchs are the guardians of the fair.

first editor of the texts, because an edition prepared by Lessing was posthumously published in the same year.[1] Both, of course, were concerned, as were other eighteenth-century antiquaries, to challenge Vasari's account of the origin of painting in oils, and their links with the study of illumination were tenuous.

[1] See Dr. C. R. Dodwell's Introduction to *Theophilus: the Various Arts*, 1961, pp. liv–lv.

III *Francis Douce ◇ his early career ◇ his post at the British Museum ◇ retirement and death ◇ his correspondence ◇ his notebooks ◇ acquisitions of manuscripts*

IN my view this important collector merits a chapter to himself. His life-span (1757–1834) places him in the middle of our period, and his outlook and accomplishments give him a transitional role in contemporary connoisseurship. His pre-eminence as an antiquary and the learned purposes for which he collected suggest affinities with his senior friend Joseph Strutt and others of that generation. On the other hand, his work on the Lansdowne and Harleian manuscripts in the British Museum gave him an eye for artistic quality in illumination of all periods which was uncommon in his era; and in the acquisition of some superlative examples of book-painting of the twelfth and thirteenth centuries he was ahead of his time. Moreover, the existence of both his collections and his personal papers and correspondence in the Bodleian Library enables us to study him in some detail.

Douce's collections were the subject of a centenary number of the *Bodleian Quarterly Record* in 1934,[1] and here we must confine ourselves mainly to the illuminated manuscripts. Very little, however, has been written hitherto on the personality of this strange, neurotic man, with a temper 'constitutionally irritable',[2] but capable of stealthy actions of great generosity: and perusal of many of his papers has led me to try to transform into a human being what to most readers is a Bodleian press-mark.

In two letters to Sir Thomas Phillipps[3] of 26 and 29 July 1831 Francis Douce gave some genealogical information relating to his family. He was the youngest of four children of Francis Douce of the

[1] Vol. vii, No. 81, pp. 359–82, a series of studies by several hands of different aspects of Douce's connoisseurship, to which I am much indebted.

[2] *Gentleman's Magazine*, N.S. ii (1834), p. 216; other unidentified quotations come from this obituary.

[3] Bodleian Library, Phillipps Correspondence, 1831 Box.

Six Clerks' Office, and his wife Ellen Tapley. In retrospect his childhood was not particularly happy. 'My grandfather', he said, 'was a domestic despot, and tyrannized over my father, who thought proper to retaliate upon me.' His mother he always mentioned with affection, and it was she who seems to have promoted his passionate early interest in books and antiquities, and especially his lifelong love of music. The latter seems to have received some paternal discouragement. 'Don't let the boy spoil the piano' is Francis Douce senior's recorded comment. Another boyhood interest which stayed with Douce all his life was angling.

He was first sent to a school at Richmond, where he learned Latin, but, he used to allege, little else. He was even more contemptuous of his next school, 'a French academy, kept by a pompous and ignorant Life-Guardsman'. It was his father's intention that he should learn book-keeping in preparation for a commercial career, but 'merchants' accounts were his aversion'. To his enduring chagrin he was not allowed to go to a university, but instead entered Gray's Inn on 13 January 1779, being subsequently admitted an attorney of the King's Bench.

On 2 November 1791 he married Isabella, widow of the Revd. Henry Price, 'late of Bellevue in Ireland'. The marriage was childless, and all contemporary witnesses agree that it was unproductive of much happiness. 'Some peculiarities of disposition in the partner of his choice occasionally embittered his life', wrote his obituarist, and there is evidence that the lady could make herself very disagreeable to her husband's antiquarian friends. Her death in 1830 was the occasion for some rather tepid expressions of condolence. At this distance, however, we must not take sides; nor must we forget that Mrs. Douce belonged to that sorely tried category, the wives of collectors. Douce only became a man of substantial means right at the end of his life, and all his resources seem to have been lavished on his collections, for which his houses in Upper Gower Street and later in Charlotte Street must have been quite inadequate. It was not as though Douce stopped short at acquiring 13,000 printed books and 400 manuscripts; his diary of accessions[1] reveals a stream of

[1] Douce MSS. e. 66–8, 'Collecta'.

antiquarian objects of all kinds. And if Mrs. Douce did not look askance at an 'ancient rolling pin' or parts of the painted rood-screen from Southwold, she may have been less acquiescent in giving house-room to 'parts of a mummied Ibis, and a piece of the outer painted coating of a human mummy', a 'Gnostic crocodile', or a plaster cast of a hermaphrodite.

For a period Douce was employed in the government office of his father, who died in 1799, the year in which he also lost his mother. The size of his legacy was a source of embitterment to him, and he complained to his friends that a large part of his share had been diverted from him by the machinations of his eldest brother, Thomas, who had persuaded his father that money left to the third son, Francis, would be squandered on books. Thereafter Douce had little other than formal contact with the rest of his family. Seeking to earn his living in a way more congenial to him, he was recruited to the staff of the Department of Manuscripts at the British Museum in 1807, and succeeded the philologist, Robert Nares, as Keeper.[1] At the Museum he worked on the catalogues of the Lansdowne and Harleian manuscripts, and it is agreed that he performed his duties conscientiously and well. Certainly the handling of hundreds of manuscripts sharpened his own critical faculties and contributed to his education as a collector. Douce, however, was one of those men who work best in solitude, and he obviously found the routine of the Museum irksome. He became head of his Department, remarked his friend Dibdin, too late in life, 'when his habits were fixed, and when even the semblance of a superior was obnoxious to him', and in another passage Dibdin recorded that 'he would neither bend nor bow to any man breathing—freedom of thought and action was his birthright, and he was determined to show it upon all occasions'.[2]

Douce was a man morbidly introspective, and in two or three of the relatively small crises in his quiet life he took a notebook and

[1] I am much indebted to Dr. C. E. Wright for examining on my behalf the records of the Department of Manuscripts, to establish exactly when Douce joined the Museum staff. He appears to have been brought in to arrange and catalogue the Lansdowne MSS., bought in 1807, and papers relating to his work on them form B.M. Add. MS. 42574. Isaac D'Israeli's letter of congratulation at his appointment was written on 15 Aug. 1807 (Bodl. MS. Douce d. 33, ff. 37–8).

[2] *Reminiscences of a Literary Life*, ii, 1836, p. 763.

recorded the facts and his emotions. To this habit we owe a blow-by-blow account of his resignation from the Museum.[1] As a document, it is so revealing of Douce's character that I propose to deal with the episode at a length which some may regard as disproportionate. The occasion of the trouble was a request from the Trustees for a report on the work of a Mr. Bean, an assistant posted to his Department apparently against his wish, but it is evident that Douce had long been brooding on various injustices, real or imagined,[2] and that the Bean episode had released a pent-up flow of complaints of all kinds.

Notes & memorandums relating to my resignation

Reasons.

1. The nature of the constitution of the M[useum] altogether objectionable.
2. The coldness, and even danger, in frequenting the great house in winter.
3. The vastness of the business remaining to be done & continually flowing in.
4. The total impossibility of my individual efforts, limited, restrained & controuled as they are, to do any real, or at least much, good.
5. An apparent, & I believe real, system of espionage throughout the place & certainly a want of due respect towards & confidence in the officers.
6. The total absence of all aid in my department.
7. The apartments I reside in are dangerously cold in winter & like an oven in summer. The whole damp, especially the lower room where my books are in great jeopardy & which I never entered, even in summer time, without being sensibly affected with some kind of pain or unpleasant sensation.
8. The general unwholesomeness of the air from sinks, drains, the ill-contrived & filthy water closet; & most of all the large & excessively cold bed chamber with an opening to the back kitchen & all its damp & cellar like smells.
9. The want of society with the members, their habits wholly different & their manners far from fascinating & sometimes repulsive.

[1] Douce MS. e. 28.

[2] Douce had been particularly incensed by the decision of the Trustees in 1810 that the catalogue of the Lansdowne MSS. should be printed by the Public Record Commissioners.

10. The want of power to do any good, & the difficulty of making the motley & often trifling committees sensible that they could do any.
11. The general pride & affected consequence of these committees.
12. Their assumption of power, that I think not vested in them.
13. Their fiddle faddle requisition of incessant reports, the greatest part of which can inform them of nothing, or, when they do, of what they are generally incapable of understanding or fairly judging of.
14. And lastly, the imperative, foolish & inconsiderate order that I should report on what Mr. Bean, no real auxiliary to me & who had no business in the house, was doing.

It is greatly to the Museum authorities' credit, I think, that after this onslaught on the Trustees, his colleagues, and the conditions of service and residence, every attempt was made to calm Douce's ruffled feelings and to persuade him to withdraw his resignation—eloquent testimony to the high regard in which his work was held. The storm blew up on 24 March 1811, when Douce was already drawing up his long memorandum. On that day the Chairman of the Trustees, Sir Joseph Banks, came to see him on other business and Douce took the opportunity to read his paper to him with much emphasis, concluding, he said, with the remark: 'I am *not to be ordered*.' Banks was conciliatory and promised to raise the complaints at the next meeting of the Trustees. In the meantime he hoped that Douce would not think of resignation, because he was irreplaceable. He made, reported Douce, 'many speeches of a consolatory purpose, partly sincere, & partly in his usual sly & courtierlike manner'. Douce continued the attack, and Banks listened patiently and admitted that certain new regulations 'had totally destroyed the pleasure he had felt before in attending to the duties of a Trustee'.

On 5 April Joseph Planta, the Principal Librarian, visited Douce and asked for the offending report on Mr. Bean. Douce having said that he would speak his mind on the subject to the Trustees, Planta generously offered to write the report himself, but at this point Douce disclosed his determination to resign, whereupon Planta quitted him 'apparently embarrassed, but with much kindness & civility'. Douce sent in his resignation on 6 April,[1] purely on grounds

[1] The text is in B.M. Add. MS. 42574, ff. 20–3.

of ill health, and after a meeting of the Trustees Banks came to express their unanimous regret, and to offer him his own terms for remaining. During the next few days several of the officers added their pleas to those of Banks. Visits were received from the Keeper of Printed Books, Henry Ellis, his assistant Henry Baber, and Douce's friend Roger Wilbraham, 'put up to pleading by Sir Joseph Banks'. Planta put in hand the repairs to Douce's apartments and 'offered some apology & explanation about Mr. Bean'. On 11 May, when the Trustees next met, Ellis called again and marshalled once more all the arguments, 'the sincerity of which might be doubted', Douce added rather ungenerously, 'when they were followed with a disclosure, in confidence, of his wish to succeed me & put Baber in his own place'. On 12 May Banks once again repeated the Trustees' resolve to meet Douce's wishes in any way possible, but he was adamant. 'My mind was made up & I acted accordingly with firmness. The fact was that my health had been injured by residing at this place, the habitation being excessively cold, damp & unwholesome & this decided me.' On reading this document, in which Douce, with an eye to posterity, has put the best face on his conduct, it is difficult to feel that he behaved quite as impeccably as he would have us believe, and, doubtless, believed himself.

He was in fact a hypersensitive man; and in 1811 he was still smarting from an affront three years old, the scars of which he bore all his life. I have dealt with this episode elsewhere,[1] and it need only be briefly summarized here: it is the subject of another agonizedly introspective notebook among his papers.[2] In 1807 he had published his most admired work, the fruit of twenty-five years of research, *Illustrations of Shakespeare and of Ancient Manners*. With one exception, reviews had been highly favourable. Most unhappily, in 1808 the *Edinburgh Review* was conducting a feud with Douce's publisher, Longman, and in this campaign Douce's book was a casualty. It received a vituperative notice, the most offensive passages in which were certainly written by the editor, Francis Jeffrey. 'Grovelling

[1] 'The Pains of Authorship: Francis Douce and the *Edinburgh Review*', in *Eighteenth-Century Studies in honor of Donald F. Hyde*, ed. W. H. Bond, New York, 1970.

[2] Douce MS. d. 58.

transcribers of black letter', 'petty antiquarians', 'laborious trifling', 'ponderous feebleness'—these and similar phrases were calculated to wound an author far less sensitive than Douce. To a man of his temperament their effect was annihilating. Page after page of his notebook was filled with draft replies and outraged expostulation. 'The disgust he conceived at the wanton and unmerited attack made upon his first publication', wrote his obituarist in 1834, 'influenced him to publish no more,[1] and it is still more to be lamented that it should have led to the sealing up of his literary remains until the close of the present century.'

After his retirement from the British Museum Douce lived quietly and frugally, immersed in his collections, his library, and his antiquarian researches. He was something of a hypochondriac, and showed an increasing reluctance to travel or even to dine out: and in an age when hard drinking was the general custom he confined himself to a single glass of madeira. He was, said a contemporary, 'a perfect gentleman of the old school (Plate 6), reserved on first acquaintance, but, when this was passed, easy, affable, kind, and alive to the common courtesies of life'. The acid comments with which he annotated his notebooks and correspondence certainly suggest a curmudgeonly disposition, and he was by nature 'suspicious of motives', but his natural politeness often concealed his inner exasperation. He was always accessible to serious scholars and his antiquarian correspondence was very large.

In 1821 he moved to 34 Kensington Square. In a letter to Dawson Turner of 4 September of that year he acknowledged the receipt of an ivory chest,[2] 'the most *amorous* of its kind that I have yet seen', and proceeded to give a rather melancholy account of his health and straitened circumstances.

You say I have no children; would to God that I had such as you have and a fortune adequate to this happiness. But of both these blessings I am deprived, and you mistake greatly . . . in supposing that I possess the means of indulging in those *modern* luxuries that you allude to. The little

[1] He in fact put his name to the long learned Introduction he wrote for William Pickering's edition of *The Dance of Death*, 1833.

[2] Trinity College, Cambridge, O. 13. 22^{50}.

fortune with which I retired from a detested profession some 20 years since has intermediately undergone no increase whatever or is likely to do so. I have therefore, oppressed by the change of times and the misconduct of rulers, been compelled to endure privations to which I had not before been accustomed: but I will not molest you with these to you uninteresting matters.

Financially, however, a dramatic improvement in Douce's circumstances was imminent. In 1823 Joseph Nollekens, the sculptor, died, and Douce was one of three residuary legatees. The will, with its fourteen codicils, was of great complexity, and the granting of probate delayed by various Dutch claimants who appeared with Nollekens pedigrees, and a Chancery suit instituted by a disappointed legatee, John Thomas Smith, formerly the sculptor's assistant and later his candid and malicious biographer. 'That serpentine miscreant' was Douce's name for him. The uncertainty of the outcome and the attendant publicity sorely tried both Douce and another of the residuary legatees, Thomas Kerrich, but in the event the legal issues were decided in their favour, largely through the skill of their lawyer, James Heywood Markland (1788–1864), a member of the Roxburghe Club. Douce's share of Nollekens's estate was about £50,000, and thereafter he was able to buy the finest manuscripts which came on to the market. The celebrated Apocalypse, for example, was acquired right at the end of his life. In other respects his wealth came too late to bring much happinesss with it; Dibdin asserted that 'his peace of mind was broken and his serenity a good deal ruffled by the Nollekens legacy', and he quotes a sad letter written to him by Douce on 26 April 1828. 'How strangely things go in this incomprehensible world! You keep up your spirits amidst occasional adversity. I lose mine in the bosom of that *prosperity* which men falsely call *happiness*.'[1]

Douce himself died in 1834, and his will also was not without its singularities, enjoining, in its opening clause, one of his executors, Sir Anthony Carlisle, Professor of Anatomy at the Royal Academy, either to behead him or remove his heart to avoid any possibility of

[1] *Reminiscences*, ii, p. 765.

premature burial.[1] He died, recorded Madden in his journal, 'quite like a Philosopher of the Stoic School—he admitted not a soul to his bedside, but ordered the curtains to be drawn, and in the presence of none but his Maker breathed his last'; and Dibdin, who viewed the body, commented on the sternness of its countenance. Such was the source of the most valuable single accession of manuscripts, books, prints and drawings ever to be received by the Bodleian; the last two classes were transferred to the Ashmolean Museum in 1863.[2] Douce's personal papers also, left to the British Museum and sealed up until 1 January 1900, by an enlightened decision have nearly all been transferred to Oxford. Only the miscellaneous antiquities, including such treasures as a superb series of medieval ivories and Holbein's miniatures of Henry VIII and Anne of Cleves, have been dispersed.[3]

When the chest of papers was opened at the British Museum in 1900, 'nothing of great interest was revealed', wrote A. H. Bullen in the *Dictionary of National Biography*, and one would like to know exactly what he had expected, or perhaps one should ask the question, 'of interest to whom?'. Here are to be found the stores of learning accumulated over a lifetime by the leading antiquary of his age, who published almost nothing—his collections on the *Gesta Romanorum*,[4] calendars and almanacs,[5] his dictionary of games,[6] alphabetical collections ranging from Abbatial Chairs to Zodiacal Memoranda,[7] his notebooks on romances,[8] fools and jesters,[9] and fairies,[10] to mention almost a random sampling.

[1] This sombre directive reflects an apprehension not uncommon at this date. See John Snart's *Thesaurus of Horror; or the Charnel-House explored*, 1817.

[2] See K. T. Parker, *Catalogue of the Collection of Drawings in the Ashmolean Museum*, 2 vols., Oxford, 1938–56. In his introductions Sir Karl points out that as a collector of drawings Douce had a strong predilection for the artists of the Northern Schools over the Italian, and that he collected as a 'scholar and antiquary rather than an enthusiast of the beautiful for its own sake'. He also draws attention to Douce's 'special delight in works whose "primitive" qualities struck him as droll and entertaining'.

[3] Bequeathed to Sir Samuel Rush Meyrick (1783–1848), the authority on armour, who published a catalogue in seven instalments in *The Gentleman's Magazine*, 1836.

[4] Douce MSS. d. 54–5 and e. 38–40.

[5] Douce MS. e. 20.

[6] Douce MS. d. 49.

[7] Douce MSS. d. 84/1–3.

[8] Douce MSS. d. 52–3 and e. 52.

[9] Douce MS. e. 26.

[10] Douce MSS. e. 99–103 and MS. f. 18.

For students of connoisseurship of the half century beginning in 1780 the correspondence is a mine of information on the antiquaries and collectors, the auctioneers and dealers of the period. In common with most of his contemporaries Douce found the bookselling house of Rodd notable for its fair dealing, and both Thomas Rodd and his brother Horatio were recipients of small legacies under his will. In 1825 he lent them a substantial sum in response to a frank and sensitive letter,[1] which contrasted favourably with that in which their rival, Thomas Thorpe, sought a loan from Douce five years later. Thorpe, whose attempts to corner the manuscript market with inadequate capital ended in disaster, was uniformly unpopular with collectors and dealers alike, and his letter received a sharp endorsement in Douce's hand:[2]

> Independently of the great impropriety of a tradesman's application to a customer for a loan of money, this man is wholly unworthy of that accommodation from those who are obliged, when they want any books of him they cannot obtain elsewhere, to employ him. He is a professed monopolizer at all sales and has more than once deservedly suffered for this illiberal conduct to gentlemen. His charges are excessive, & his constant procession of catalogues, not to be accounted for on fair principles, are absolutely annoying. I have always paid him immediately without requiring the discount which he ought to have allowed, even without the hint I have more than once given him & he had not the wit to see that herein he is standing in his own light. I have not thought him deserving of pity when I have found him marking books in his catalogues at much less than he had wantonly given for them.

With the gentlemanly firm of Payne and Foss, Douce, as was to be expected, had many cordial transactions, but he failed to take advantage of perhaps his most outstanding opportunity to buy a printed book of superlative rarity, when on 12 January 1825 they offered him the first quarto of *Hamlet*, 1603.[3] Among the auctioneers, James Christie provides a series of learned and interesting letters, though some give a rather disconcerting picture of sale-room attributions. 'Be assured', wrote the auctioneer on 11 June 1808, 'that you

[1] Douce MS. d. 28, f. 13.
[2] Douce MS. d. 27, f. 86.
[3] Douce MS. d. 25, f. 9.

have not missed any very precious relick of antiquity in losing the Altarpiece bought by Somers, which was not painted by L. da Vinci, but by honest Lucas of Leyden whose works may be frequently picked up for less than he gave for the picture in question.'[1]

The letters from antiquaries and bibliographers include long series from Francis Grose, William Herbert, and the irrepressible George Steevens, and indeed it is not easy to think of an antiquary unrepresented; Thomas Pennant, Richard Gough, Joseph Ritson, George Chalmers, John Brand, John Pinkerton—they are all there. Among letters of book collectors, I wish to quote from one written by that great collector of romances and translator of Froissart, Thomas Johnes of Hafod. It was written on 16 March 1817, when he had just received news of the disastrous fire which had destroyed his house and library, and was about to hurry from London to Wales to inspect the damage and rejoin his family, who had barely escaped with their lives. One cannot but admire the spirit with which Johnes reported the disaster and then added:

> Now, my dear Sir, I hope what I am going to add you will not think impertinence, indeed I do not mean it, but you complained yesterday so justly of the times, that perhaps you may wish to increase your income, and as I have lost my library, or at least great part of it, should you be inclined to part with yours, or what you may wish to separate from it, I shall think myself very much obliged to be allowed to become the purchaser of the whole or of part.[2]

In an endorsement Douce drafted a reply 'to this precipitate and rather indelicate application'. After expressing his grief at the catastrophe, so poignant that he had refused an invitation to dine out on that evening, he continued: 'I know, my dear Sir, that whenever you may have leisure for a little reflexion you will adopt exactly the same feelings for the situation which I should be placed in deprived of so large a portion of my happiness & amusement as the sacrifice of my books would be. *I* have no *child* to console me for such a loss ...' The financial setbacks he had suffered, he affirmed, were not on a scale which necessitated his considering Johnes's proposal, which,

[1] Douce MS. d. 21, f. 171.

[2] Douce MS. d. 23, ff. 39–40.

he thought, did not in fact emanate from Johnes himself, but had been suggested by a third party, 'a man devoid of any delicacy, . . . who would himself convert any thing he possesses into money, if he could gain a tradesman's profit on it; whom, were he to urge the matter again, I should inform that no change of time or circumstance would ever induce me to act as some of his rash & imprudent friends have done'.

Among the longer correspondences is a lively series of letters from George Hardinge (1743–1816),[1] Horace Walpole's 'out-pensioner of Bedlam' and neighbour at Twickenham. Hardinge, a breathless gossipy correspondent, laid down the law on Shakespearean matters in general and on Edmund Malone in particular. Another attractive series of letters is from Douce's warm friend, Roger Wilbraham (1743–1829),[2] the wealthy bachelor whose life revolved round the pleasures of the table, the shooting field, and his splendid library, pre-eminent in Italian books. Wilbraham writes friendly letters, full of literary gossip on romances, Shakespeare, early carols, Italian literature, and Ugo Foscolo.

Another close friend was Thomas Kerrich (1748–1828), Librarian of the University of Cambridge, a distinguished antiquary and a talented amateur painter and etcher. The two collectors exchanged information continuously about prints, and Kerrich listed for Douce all his own engraved works. There are many references, too, to Kerrich's posthumously published catalogue of the prints of Heemskerck, 'a pretty little daudling amusement for old age', as the compiler described it. There is an interesting letter[3] of 7 November 1805, in which Kerrich expatiates at some length and in some detail on the special difficulties which confront the historian of painting in Britain. On 5 December 1825 he blows rather cold on the abilities of a figure of whom I shall have a good deal to say later, William Young Ottley, commended to him by Douce.

If Mr. Ottley be a man of such great Abilities [replied Kerrich], why does he throw them away on Inventories, & Dictionaries of mere Copying Clerks (for I look upon Engravers to be little better), & making lumbering books about the origin of engraving? Proper employment for Messrs.

[1] Douce MS. c. 6. [2] Douce MS. d. 40. [3] Douce MS. d. 36, f. 22.

Bartsch & Basan, & Papillon, &c., &c. Publishing accurate prints from *important* Pictures, whether that importance consists in *intrinsic* or *extrinsic* merit—I hold to be very good—but I own that I do hate a heavy book should be tacked to their tail. Hamilton's Scuola Italica I delight in on this account: he had join'd no nonsense of his own to it.[1]

A letter from Kerrich of 8 May 1808 reveals a piece of academic snobbery of interest to Cambridge librarians. 'Mr. Lysons tells me that John Bowtell, a very good bookbinder of this place, was proposed at the Society of Antiquaries last Thursday, to be Fellow of it; & that they had the impudence to call him "John Bowtell, Esquire." If they like to elect Bookbinders or Shoemakers I cannot help it, but I do think it my duty to let you know (& them through you) that I know the man very well, & that he is no Esquire, but a mere Bookbinder—& in his business has great merit.'[2] Librarians today who ruefully contemplate rows of medieval manuscripts tightly rebound by Bowtell in undistinguished calf may dissent from Kerrich's view of Bowtell's professional standing, but it is sad to record that the Society of Antiquaries, unlike the *Dictionary of National Biography*, did not open its doors to the historian of the town of Cambridge and its generous benefactor.

The correspondence, however, which shows Douce in a very favourable light is the 187-page series of letters from T. F. Dibdin extending from 1806 to 1834. Douce, although sorely tried by Dibdin's fatuity and his importunate pleas for money, proved a generous friend to him in adversity. Dibdin usually wanted something when he wrote—Douce's support for his candidature as Secretary of the Society of Antiquaries or Librarian of the London Institution, a subscription to one of his works, a favourable review for *The Bibliographical Decameron*, a loan of £1,500, or some leaves from Douce's copy of Caxton's *Golden Legend* to perfect that of his patron, Lord Spencer. In most cases, including the last, Douce complied, and gave vent to his irritation in tart annotations. 'In consequence of this jackal rhapsody', he wrote in reference to the Caxton, 'I presented the leaves in question (the most important part of the book) to the noble Lord, who very nobly thanked me some time

[1] Douce MS. d. 36, f. 293.

[2] Douce MS. d. 21, f. 167.

afterwards in person & afterwards by his said jackal most nobly presented me with a print which I had previously bought for a shilling. This Caxton was increased at least £100 in value by the addition of the prologue and the cut belonging to it. I very modestly asked afterwards for a drawing of the cut but never obtained it.'[1]

It is difficult to decide whether some of the Doctor's letters are written in his normal condition of euphoric facetiousness or in drink, and certainly several give the latter impression. The announcement of the Nollekens legacy in 1823 was the occasion of what Douce described as 'a very silly, rattling, Dibdinical letter!' But thereafter he made Dibdin loans without hope of return, attempted to advise him on his intricately involved finances, and only occasionally jibbed at the rather pathetic attempts Dibdin made from time to time to pay his debts in kind. On 7 September 1830, for example, Douce was sent a Limoges enamel crucifix with the request to 'keep it as a *little* bit of makeweight in my Credit . . . Jarman tells me it was obtained at Paris for 750 francs.' 'Jarman is a liar. It is not worth 40 francs', is Douce's endorsement, and he returned the 'commonplace and hideous' crucifix, adding to his private note: 'In this way does this poor embarrassed man make good his promises to repay his loans. God help him, if helped he can be.'[2]

To Dibdin's face, however, these asperities were less apparent, and Douce continued to lend him books, and even manuscripts to be copied for engraving in his publications, to forgive him his debts, and finally to bequeath him a very welcome legacy of £500—striking confirmation of the phrase in Douce's obituary which refers to his 'constant and unvariable attachment to those whom he had once admitted into the circle of his friends'.

Douce was an exceptionally methodical man and, as was to be expected, his papers provide a good deal of documentation on the history of his library. Moreover his habit of annotation caused him to add the flesh of comment and anecdote to the skeleton of mere lists. A case in point is MS. Douce e. 75, a notebook in which he kept a record of books lent, lost, or mislaid, and in which he apportioned blame to casual borrowers or (less often) praise to punctilious ones.

[1] Douce MS. d. 32, f. 164.

[2] Douce MS. d. 32, ff. 99–100.

Among the black sheep were Thorkelin, Dibdin, Ottley, and (needless to say) Porson; whereas in a class labelled 'most scrupulous, careful and punctual' are to be found Sir Joseph Banks, Malone, and Isaac D'Israeli. The same notebook contains a few petulant pages of 'Instances of liberality in some book collectors', in which Douce again records his dislike of Lord Spencer.

I had most fortunately acquired [he noted] 2 of the very curious slips of Caxton's book advertisement stuck up by him in the printing office at the Almonry. I shewed these to Edwards who told Lord S. of them & he delegated the artful Yorkshireman to negotiate an exchange. Now as there is no 3d. specimen of the kind existing one of these was at least equal in value to one of the books printed by Caxton, & so Edwards admitted. A copy of the Virgil & an old dotted print were proposed in exchange to which I consented & delivered one of the above slips. When I examined the Virgil I found it wanted the prologue. Notwithstanding this I afterwards heard that the Lord was not satisfied with the exchange, when I voluntarily gave him a very fine & perfect copy of a Lyndewode by W. de Worde, when he somewhat indecorously said to me 'Aye this is something'. I was almost tempted to remonstrate on the imperfection of his Virgil, but was not certain that he was aware of it, though I think his Yorkshire agent must have been.[1]

In spite of these splenetic utterances there is plenty of evidence that Douce lent books and manuscripts freely all his life, even ones of high value. Another of his notebooks is devoted to 'Books Sold',[2] and is of interest from the scale of operations it reveals. Douce was by no means a 'crypto-bookseller', but his constant urge to buy better copies, and his purchases of multi-volume lots at sales, caused him to amass duplicates which were systematically discarded in the auction room or sent to his regular booksellers to be credited to his account. Between July 1799 and December 1805, for example, eleven such transactions took place, nor were only printed books involved. At Leigh and Sotheby's auction of 24 August 1800 he included a tenth-century text of St. Augustine's Homilies, but noted against it 'Bought again'; five years later he was allowed £2. 2*s*. 0*d*. for it in an exchange of books with Benjamin White, of Fleet Street. Another

[1] Douce MS. e. 75, f. 15.

[2] Douce MS. d. 62.

of Douce's acts of unobtrusive kindness is recorded here. When young Joseph Strutt, son of the engraver, left Hansard's printing house to set up as a bookseller in Middle Row, Holborn, Douce let him have a number of books on sale or return to fill his shelves, 'having a very good opinion of his integrity & obliging disposition as well as respect for the memory of his father'; and when shortly afterwards the new bookseller failed, Douce presented him with all the unsold books.

Another series of small notebooks, 'Libri Ligat.',[1] should bring a gleam to the eye of the historian of bookbinding. In these Douce records, with the binders' names, all the volumes he had bound for him from 1797 until his death in 1834. His first binder was Barrett, on whose death in 1798 he moved to Hering, whom he patronized exclusively until 1804. Thereafter until 1825 he shared his custom among half a dozen firms, and during the last nine years of his life he dealt solely with the bindery of Besant.

In one respect, however, and that an important one, the documentation relating to the collections is disappointing. The three notebooks labelled 'Collecta',[2] Douce's records of accessions, are scrappy, incomplete, and tantalizing, because often the entries are too cryptic to admit of exact identification (Plate 7). They run from 1803 to 1834, and it is salutory to recall, especially in the earlier years, how many things other than books and manuscripts Douce collected. 'Chinese cards, ear instruments, shop bills, musk cake, Auction at King's' is a typical entry (January 1803): and at this period coins loom the largest in the accession-lists. Many gifts are recorded—of medals from Flaxman, drawings from Cosway, prints and antiquities from John Brand, Thomas Stothard, and others. Many of his friends' publications, of course, feature, mainly antiquarian but sometimes of wider interest. Isaac D'Israeli presented his literary works, Samuel Rogers his *Pleasures of Memory*, and Walter Scott a large-paper copy of his life of Dryden. Some very valuable articles came to Douce by gift. In 1790, for example, George Steevens gave him MS. Douce 175, the Romance of the Sowdon of Babyloyne; in March 1804 Taylor Combe, the numismatist, a 'MS. of medicine

[1] Douce MSS. e. 71–3.

[2] Douce MSS. e. 66–8.

and poetry, temp. H[enry] 6'; and in June 1810 'Mr. Alexander gave me the valuable MS. of the romance of King Horn, the fables of Marie etc. A very precious gift.' This last is MS. Douce 132, a thirteenth-century volume which contains, as well as the texts mentioned, another romance and an illustrated Bestiary. Other medieval manuscripts were presents from Roger Wilbraham, E. V. Utterson, Henry Ellis, and David Laing. In 1823 Douce entered up the gift of 'Mr. Singer's inestimable volume of small drawings by Le petit Bernard'. This was Samuel Weller Singer (1783–1858), the historian of playing-cards and a life-long friend and correspondent, to whom Douce left a legacy which enabled him to retire from the librarianship of the Royal Institution.

Douce's manuscript acquisitions before 1803, when his register began, can in some measure be studied from inscriptions in the books themselves, or from a number of annotated sale catalogues which he bound into volumes. When he was nineteen he bought two manuscripts at the sale of the library of Dr. John Campbell in May 1776, a fourteenth-century French chronicle of England (MS. 120) and a fifteenth-century volume containing Vegetius and other works (MS. 147). In the following year he attended the sale of the library of John Ives on 3 March and noted in his catalogue several purchases by John Jackson, Richard Gough, and Joseph Ritson.[1] It is also interesting to observe that at twenty years of age he was beginning to indulge in those tart marginalia which are such a feature of his books. When the cataloguer, against lot 412, printed Ives's commendatory note on the quality of the miniatures of a Roman Missal, young Douce responded 'a most ignorant & silly note as all written by this gentleman were'. The well-thumbed pages of his catalogue[2] of Mark Cephas Tutet's sale of 15 February 1786 attest the assiduity with which he viewed that remarkable collection of early printing, bibliography, and a few choice manuscripts; and an occasional annotation brings the scene to life, as when, for instance, Gough with a five-guinea bid wins lot 55, 'Two volumes of antient and modern cards', against the competition of Horace Walpole.

[1] Douce CC 295 (2). [2] Douce CC 295 (6).

At the anonymous sale of Count MacCarthy's books which began on 18 May 1789 Douce bought no less than eighteen manuscripts[1] for a total of £26. 18*s*. 6*d*. Another sale at which he was very active was that of the late Gustavus Brander, F.R.S., of Christchurch, Hampshire, held by Leigh and Sotheby on 8 February 1790, the source of at least eleven lots of medieval manuscripts and charters,[2] including lot 1,153, Sanctorum Vitae, which Douce noted as being 'very antient & curious', and which may perhaps be identified with MS. 174, a fine eleventh-century book with illuminated capitals.

One of the most rewarding volumes of catalogues is Douce CC. 393, a collection of sixteen sales between 1791 and 1807, a high proportion of considerable interest, including the libraries of Francis Grose, John Jackson, Samuel Ireland, John Wilkes, two sales of Joseph Ritson's books (one anonymous), Bridgewater and Spencer duplicates, William Herbert's manuscripts, and a monastic library of incunabula from Bamberg. At John Jackson's sale on 28 April 1794 Douce bought six manuscripts for a total of £15. 17*s*. 0*d*., one of them the admired eleventh-century Psalter (MS. 296), with a fine Beatus leaf and full-page miniature of the Winchester School (lot 368). A manuscript with so little decoration cannot have seemed cheap at £5. 10*s*. 0*d*., but it was in fine condition, unlike lot 346, Piers Plowman (MS. 104), with marginal illustrations, which cost Douce £1. 5*s*. 0*d*. At the sale of Herbert's manuscripts, held by the obscure auctioneers Arrowsmith and Bowley on 21 November 1798, Douce laid out £2. 17*s*. 0*d*. on four manuscripts, including two copies of the Pricke of Conscience (lots 948 and 949).

In December 1801 Douce bought one of his greatest bargains, at the sale of the library of the late Samuel Tyssen, F.S.A., of Narborough Hall, Norfolk. Lot 2526 was a book which had already been expensive in the seventeenth century, a seventh/eighth-century Hiberno-Saxon text of Primasius on the Apocalypse (MS. 140). An inserted leaf from a library catalogue of the late seventeenth century, perhaps of Walter Clavell, contains the volume priced at £26. 17*s*. 0*d*. Joseph Ames subsequently owned it, had his name stamped on the seventeenth-century binding, and referred to it in his *History of*

[1] Marked in Douce CC 301 (1).

[2] See Douce CC 297 (7).

Printing.[1] At his sale in 1760 Mark Cephas Tutet gave £10. 10*s*. 0*d*. for it, and at *his* sale in 1786 Tyssen bought it for £8. Small wonder that when Douce bought this, his earliest manuscript, for a paltry £2. 9*s*. 0*d*.,[2] he noted with satisfaction on the fly-leaf 'Not the tenth part of its value'.

From 1803 we can learn the source of some, but by no means all, of Douce's most important purchases. 'I got a magnificent Italian Ceremoniale of Payne and Mackinlay',[3] he recorded in June 1804, 'in exchange for the chronicle printed by Macklinia, which Lord Spencer took for 25 guineas, the price of the MS. It is the finest I ever saw.' In April 1807 we find him buying four manuscripts at the sale of Sir John Sebright's collections, including one with a noble provenance—Archbishop Matthew Parker, William Lambarde, and Sir Roger Twysden (MS. 128). Richard Gough's sale in 1810 was another natural source of manuscripts. In September 1812 he bought from the bookseller Triphook 'a very curious ms. of Rabanus Maurus', a thirteenth-century text with coloured figures (MS. 192). In July 1817 we may note the first record of purchase of cuttings from manuscripts, 'three small illuminations from a ms. of L[ancelot] de lac. Simco'.[4] These accessions of single miniatures continue intermittently, usually from the picture and print dealers, Colnaghi, Nosada, and others. '17 illuminations from a splendid Flemish MS. of Roman d'Hector, Colnaghi, with a Hindoo portrait and a print by Breughel' is one of the last I have noted, in February 1827. In June 1817 Payne and Foss buy six books for him at the MacCarthy sale in Paris; a year later the purchase of 'MS. Bestiaire' from Rodd's catalogue is noted (MS. 88), and Payne provided in April 1823 the fine illustrated romance of Reynard the Fox and Isengrin (MS. 360), written in 1339, and previously in the La Vallière library.

When Douce received his very large legacy from the Nollekens estate he had been collecting avidly for nearly fifty years, and it is good to observe the old man, to whom money at last was no object, rising to the occasion and finishing the course at a splendid canter,

[1] 1749 edn., p. 505.

[2] The price Douce recorded in the manuscript. In his copy of the sale catalogue (TT 147(4)) he has written £2/18/–.

[3] Unidentified.

[4] Douce MS. d. 13, fol. 2, b–d.

outstripping his competitors in the acquisition of the finest items which came on to the market.

In these last years of accessions 1829 seems to be the *annus mirabilis*. The dispersal of George Hibbert's great library[1] presented some outstanding opportunities, and at the sale, or from the booksellers after it, Douce bought two block-books, an Apocalypse (lot 410) and the former Gaignat–MacCarthy copy of *Speculum Humanae Salvationis* (lot 7588); he also acquired the grandest of his illustrated romances, a copy of the Roman de la Rose, with 125 large miniatures (lot 6947, £84). This sumptuous volume, now Douce MS. 195, had also previously belonged to MacCarthy. Again from Hibbert's collection Douce obtained a La Vallière–Towneley manuscript of the French version of Valerius Maximus, with many fine miniatures and marginal directions to the artist (MSS. 202–3), a fitting pair for a purchase from Payne two months later of the French Caesar (MS. 208), also with miniatures, formerly in the possession of Louis XIV and the Duc de La Vallière. May 1829 had seen the purchase from Bohn of 'Gospels 11th. cent. with ivory dyptic', a noble book in a contemporary binding of ivory and brass (MS. 292). In June he bought for £47. 5*s*. 0*d*., from the catalogue of John Cochran,[2] a volume of treatises, with four fine miniatures written at Ghent in 1475 for Margaret of York, Duchess of Burgundy (MS. 365); and for £15. 15*s*. 0*d*. a grandly decorated late manuscript, Marguerite de Navarre's 'La Coche ou le Debat de l'Amour' (MS. 91). This galaxy is but a selection; there were other named manuscripts, groups of early woodcut books, purchases at the Guilford sale, parcels of books from Thorpe, Lilly, and others, as well as a consignment of books imported from the Continent for Douce by Walther.

A few further accessions of the very first rank must not pass unnoted. In June 1831 Payne and Foss provided 'a splendid book of homilies with illum[ns]', the important fourteenth-century *Sermologium* from the diocese of Lake Constance (MS. 185). In November the terse entry 'Fine Norwich psalter. Thorpe' marks the arrival of one of his greatest treasures, the Ormesby Psalter (MS. 366). In June

[1] See Douce's large-paper marked copy, given him by Hibbert, Douce h. 261.

[2] Douce c. 627.

1832 he bought 'the very curious diabolical Vigne spirituelle' from Payne, a late-fifteenth-century book with horrific miniatures of high quality (MS. 134), once the property of his friend Dibdin, who reproduced two of the pictures in his *Reminiscences of a Literary Life*. In December of the same year we find an entry, 'The magnificent Missal with p[aintings] by Hans Memmling. Of M. Focken the rector of S. Ursula at Cologne', and if Focken had not been mentioned it would have been difficult correctly to identify the item with MS. 112, one of his grandest late Books of Hours, with miniatures by the Master of the David Scenes in the Grimani Breviary. In February 1833 he bought from Thorpe the most famous of all his possessions, the thirteenth-century Apocalypse, which bears his name. 'Beautiful MS. Revel[atio]ns (Wilsons)'[1] hardly does it justice (MS. 180).

The pace never slackened, right to the end. In October 1833 he bought MS. 248, a Delft Book of Hours with beautiful miniatures in grisaille, and the following month from Payne 'Lectiones 10 cent[ur]y with diptych', the very important Gospel Lectionary (MS. 176) written, later research has shown, as early as about 800 at Chelles, and adorned with a ninth-century ivory of the 'Ada School'. The final entry is at the end of February 1834, '3 or 4 Roman pottery & other stamps'. The hand is firm, and under the line Douce wrote the heading 'March', underlining the month twice, as had been his invariable practice for thirty years: but, before the March accessions could be entered up, Douce was dead.

This chapter is an attempt to make some assessment of Douce as a collector, and not to list his manuscripts, even the finest ones. Specialists will recognize many famous omissions from the individual items I have cited, starting with MS. 59, 'Codex aureus purpureus', a Rheims Psalter of the ninth century, and especially, among the numerous Books of Hours of fine quality, the Limbourg Book of 1407 (MS. 144), for example, the Hours of the Master of Mary of Burgundy (MSS. 219–20), or the Hours of Bona Sforza, painted by Stanislas Mogila in 1527–8 (MS. 40). The index of any modern work

[1] Identified by Mr. Neil Ker (*B.L.R.* v (1956), p. 283) as William Wilson, F.S.A., of the Minories.

on medieval illumination will reveal Douce's high standing. Nor should it be forgotten that Douce was foremost an antiquary, and that the majority of his manuscripts were gathered for scholarly purposes: one may instance the texts of the *Gesta Romanorum*, which he collected with the preparation of an edition in view. In his chosen fields he amassed an incomparable learned library, as one who has used his bibliography and palaeography extensively can testify.

In the section on illuminated manuscripts in the centenary number of the *Bodleian Quarterly Record* Douce is described as 'a careful and discriminating collector', and it is remarked that nearly all his illuminated manuscripts were 'of superior execution'. The annotations in his books, however, it is said, 'do not show great acuteness or wide experience of manuscripts, although for some years he had been Keeper of Manuscripts at the British Museum'. From this view I must dissent. Of course, some of his artistic judgements, especially attributions, have not stood the test of time, and Pietro Perugino is unlikely to have decorated his MS. 11, as his note suggests. In general, however, at a period when many collectors were writing arrant nonsense in their books, Douce's annotations seem to me to be unusually judicious and still worthy of consideration. His chief claim to our attention, however, must be his position as one of the earliest of those collectors who can be studied in detail, to assemble a really representative series of illuminated manuscripts of all periods, including those least fashionable in his day. In his lifetime Douce commanded respect, and his recognition of quality in unfamiliar areas of connoisseurship commands it still; it would be hard to duplicate in many of his contemporaries.

IV *A patrician provenance ◇ case-history of the Missal of Cardinal Della Rovere ◇ J. B. Jarman ◇ W. Y. Ottley ◇ the trade in single miniatures ◇ William Roscoe ◇ Thomas Coke ◇ T. F. Dibdin and* The Bibliographical Decameron *◇ his survey of manuscripts and collectors ◇ William Beckford ◇ P. A. Hanrott ◇ Viscount Fitzwilliam ◇ Sir Thomas Phillipps ◇ Thomas Grenville's* Victories of Charles V

THROUGHOUT the first three decades of the nineteenth century a gradual shifting of taste is discernible. A few collectors awakened to the attractions of miniatures of the twelfth and thirteenth centuries, but among the great majority the old-fashioned preferences still prevailed; it is almost axiomatic that the grander the collector, the less likely he was to venture outside the well-attested schools of the late fifteenth and sixteenth centuries. Provenance has always fascinated me, and down the years during which I have taken note of the ownership of manuscripts I have amused myself by looking for the book with the most patrician provenance imaginable. There is one which must come very high on the list, a manuscript which came on to the market seven times in ninety years, and, it is clear, aroused an irresistible urge for accession in the hearts of the most celebrated collectors. A list of its owners should be read to a roll of drums— Girardot de Préfond, Gaignat, the Duc de La Vallière, Crevenna, the Duke of Roxburghe, the Duke of Marlborough, Mr. John Broadley[1] and Mr. D. S. Ker[2] (a lapse from the world of the Almanac de Gotha, but only a temporary one), the Earl of Ashburnham, and

[1] F.S.A., F.L.S., editor of *Memoirs of the Life of Master John Shawe*, 1824; Evans held two sales of his library, in 1832 and 1833.

[2] David Stewart Ker (1816–78), M.P. for County Down 1852–7; his library was dispersed in four sales by Christie, 1847–9.

finally that Renaissance Prince of the New World, John Pierpont Morgan I. And what was this manuscript without which no ducal library was complete? Rather a dull one in fact, a heraldic work decorated with 175 emblazoned armorial bearings, *Noms, armes et blasons des chevaliers de la Table Ronde*, written about 1500 for Louis de Hédouville, Seigneur de Sandricourt, where a tournament was staged in 1493 (Plate 8). The book indeed has its modest place in the literature of jousting and is respectfully cited by historians.[1] In 1848 Lord Ashburnham paid £43. 1*s*. 0*d*. for it, and its price had shown no very substantial fluctuations over the previous ninety years. Why did these noble collectors brush aside all opposition to acquire this specialized text, of no more than average decoration? Was it snobbery? some passion for the genealogy of legend? Was their desire to set this volume alongside those more splendidly illuminated romances of chivalry, which it was the fashion to acquire? Certainly the book and its owners epitomize one aspect of the Gothic Revival, the aspect which induced the nobility of Britain unsuitably clad in bascinets, vambraces, cuisses, sabatons, and other ironmongery, to flounder in the mud at the Eglinton Tournament during the exceptionally wet August of 1839.

The case-history of another very-late-fifteenth-century manuscript, of much higher quality and decoration, is also worth citing, because it both illustrates the survival of the conservative elements of taste and neatly introduces several collectors who are influential in our period. Pierpont Morgan Library MS. No. 306 is a splendid Missal written and illuminated in Verona for Cardinal Domenico Della Rovere.[2] The miniatures, delicate—not to say effeminate—are the work of two hands, and one of them has the rare distinction of bearing the signature of the artist, Francischus Veronensis, now identified by art historians as Francesco de Castello (Plate 9).[3] This

[1] F. H. Cripps-Day, *The History of the Tournament in England and France*, 1918, p. 89; Edouard Sandoz, 'Tourneys in the Arthurian Tradition', *Speculum*, xix (Oct. 1944), pp. 389–420, which cites this manuscript as the source of the text, *La Forme quon tenoit des tornoys*.

[2] Seventy-three MSS. from Domenico's library are in the Archivio di Stato and the Biblioteca Nazionale at Turin: several (e.g. E. III 3 and E. III 8) are illuminated by the artist who decorated Morgan 306.

[3] The most recent literature includes: Raffaello Brenzoni, 'I due miniaturisti Veronesi del Messale di Domenico della Rovere della Pierpont Morgan Library di New York',

beautiful manuscript first appeared on the English market at a sale at Christie's on 25 April 1804. The property was anonymous and Messrs. Christie's records throw no light on the owner. An early note, however, in a copy of the catalogue in the British Museum attributes the ownership to Edward Thurlow, who succeeded to the title of 2nd Baron Thurlow in 1806. It may well be that some of the items in the catalogue were Thurlow's property, but whether he owned the whole library I venture to doubt, for it seems to be almost too remarkable a collection to have been formed and dispersed by a young man of twenty-three. Admittedly, by 1802 he had acquired four sinecures, including that of Clerk of Lunacy and of the Custody of Idiots in the Diocese of Lincoln before his fifth birthday. Christie described the collection as 'the genuine property of a gentleman of distinguished taste retiring into the country', but the sale has not an entirely homogeneous air. Thurlow, so the radical *Peerage for the People* informs us, was 'chiefly known from having married Miss Bolton, the actress, and from having been an unfortunate aspirant in verse making . . ., a propensity most unfortunate for himself, and for a whole host of creditors, to boot. The poor Lord, under perpetual apprehension of bailiffs' visits, was obliged for several years to live without having a thing about him to call his own.'[1] This, one might say, provides a grain of evidence for the forced sale of his library. It would be tempting, however, to suggest that the Missal of Cardinal Della Rovere was imported from Italy by William Young Ottley, who will figure in this chapter. Certainly at this date he had recently returned from Rome, and was dispersing at Christie's art treasures collected in Italy,[2] and the unusually sophisticated description of the manuscript in Christie's catalogue suggests Ottley's hand. But this is mere conjecture, and the problem of ownership must await the production of further evidence. The Missal's quality, however, was readily recognized, and it fetched the substantial sum of

Archivio Veneto, 5th Ser. xliv–xlv (1949), pp. 48–56; Franco Riva, 'Cimeli di Francesco dai Libri Scuola a New York e a Verona', *Arte Veneta* (1953), pp. 135–9; Raffaello Brenzoni, 'Il Messale di Domenico della Rovere nella Morgan Library di New York e il suo miniatore Francesco de Castello', *L'Arte*, lxi (1963), pp. 3–11.

1 William Carpenter, *Peerage for the People*, 1837, p. 720.

2 In particular the important sale of forty-nine pictures, held by Christie on 16 May 1801.

£131 under the hammer, being bought by the bookseller John Arch. The book appeared in John White's catalogue of January 1806, but did not find a purchaser. As late as 1814 Dibdin borrowed it from Messrs. White and Cochrane, having insured it for £450, so that engravings could be made of some of the miniatures for his projected *Bibliographical Decameron*; and when the book appeared in 1817 Dibdin devoted no less than thirteen pages to a rhapsodic description of the manuscript.[1]

Of the illuminations he wrote:

> Collectively there is nothing to be put in competition with them. Even the grotesques enhance the value of the volume; and the frequent betrayal of a remnant of what is called *Gothic taste*, connecting the old with the new school of art, gives additional interest to the performance. Yet the specimens of beautiful and even Grecian taste which prevails—the arabesque borders, now fanciful and now grave—the incrustations of gems and precious stones—the onyx, sardine, ruby, emerald, amethyst, pearl—in sundry compartments of borders, or ornaments of capital initials—these, (minor decorations, I grant) these, of their kind, know of no superiority in any contemporaneous Missal!

Between 1814 and 1816 the Missal changed hands twice. White and Cochrane sold it to Edward Astle (1770–1816), one of the nine children of Thomas Astle the palaeographer: and at the auction of his library, held by Evans on 10 January 1816, the Missal appeared as lot 246, with a full-page description, learned and ecstatic. Its value had increased dramatically since 1804, and it was bought for £304. 10*s*. 0*d*. by the print and autograph dealer, John Thane, from whose hands it passed into those of William Esdaile (1758–1837), the banker. Esdaile was mainly a collector of prints and drawings. His Rembrandt etchings and the series of Claude drawings, many from Lawrence's collection, were especially outstanding. Christie's held eight sales of Esdaile's works of art between 1838 and 1848, and the Esdaile Missal, as it was now called, was lot 358 on 15 March 1838. The slump which prevailed in the eighteen-thirties kept prices down, and the Missal was secured for £160 by the very interesting jeweller and art dealer, John Boykett Jarman.

[1] Vol. i, 1817, pp. cxlii–clv.

Jarman's activities as a collector—and indeed as a manufacturer—of medieval manuscripts have recently been learnedly and entertainingly chronicled by Miss Janet Backhouse. Her article, 'A Victorian Connoisseur and his Manuscripts: the Tale of Mr. Jarman and Mr. Wing',[1] throws light, some of it slightly horrific, on the practice of supplying missing miniatures and of retouching and restoring those damaged by the ravages of time. Ample opportunity was afforded to Jarman; for his collection of manuscripts spent three days under water during a disastrous flood in 1846, when the King's Scholars' Pond Sewer gushed into Jarman's cellars at 83 Grosvenor Street. I commend Miss Backhouse's able detective work on London drainage, which has enabled her to correct the error of Sir Sydney Cockerell (derived from Ruskin), who placed the scene of the inundation twenty miles away at Datchet. Jarman's medieval manuscripts, some of them water-stained, retouched and rebound, were sold at Sotheby's in 1864, and Miss Backhouse has supplied a very useful list of them and their present locations. They reveal Jarman, who was collecting before 1817, as a connoisseur almost entirely committed to the acquisition of late highly decorated Books of Hours. He also accumulated single miniatures and borders cut from manuscripts of the same period. This was undoubtedly his personal taste, and these late books were reserved from his stock for retention in his own collection. One very famous manuscript of the thirteenth century, however, passed through his hands in the way of business, the Psalter and Hours of Isabella of France,[2] written about 1260–70, sold to John Ruskin in 1854, and, under the misnomer of the 'St. Louis Psalter', regarded by Ruskin as his greatest treasure.

At Jarman's sale in 1864 the Missal of Cardinal Della Rovere, although sadly damaged, fetched £141. 15*s.* 0*d.*, and reached its final home in the Pierpont Morgan Library via the Rahir collection. So much for the persistence throughout the nineteenth century of the conservative and traditional pattern of connoisseurship, and its preoccupation with the most highly finished productions of the Italian Renaissance.

[1] *British Museum Quarterly*, xxxii (1968), pp. 76–92.
[2] Cambridge, Fitzwilliam Museum, MS. 300.

Already at the beginning of the century, however, schools of painting of an earlier and very different kind were gaining limited appreciation in the eyes of a few connoisseurs, whose tastes were being formed and guided by one or two exceptionally percipient dealers; and at this point we must consider at some length the career of William Young Ottley, certainly a key figure in our investigation.

Students of connoisseurship in the first three decades of the nineteenth century will find the name of Ottley constantly recurring. His publications, especially *The Italian School of Design* and his history of engraving, both pioneer works in their field, entitle him to our respect as an art historian; and his pre-eminence as a collector of drawings has been investigated by Mr. J. A. Gere.[1]

Apart from the great collection of drawings which he sold to Sir Thomas Lawrence for £8,000, he was a dealer on a very large scale. No less than twelve sales of parts of his collections are listed in Lugt's *Répertoire des Catalogues de Ventes*, and there were doubtless other anonymous ones as yet unidentified. Ottley imported many celebrated paintings into this country; Botticelli's *Nativity*, for example, in the National Gallery, passed through his hands. Art historians are well aware of Ottley's importance as one of the Englishmen most influential in the rediscovery of Italian primitives.[2] Ownership of such works as Ugolino's altar panels, painted at Siena about 1300, reveals a remarkable change from traditional connoisseurship in the earliest years of the nineteenth century, and his role in these developments has received due recognition. Ottley interests us as a man who saw clearly that medieval miniatures belonged to the history of painting.

Ottley, born in 1771, was the son of an officer in the Coldstream Guards and was educated at Winchester. Having studied at the Royal Academy Schools, he went to Italy in 1791 and stayed there for the ten most formative years of his life, collecting paintings, drawings and miniatures in the chaotic and opportune conditions which

[1] *British Museum Quarterly*, xvii (1952), pp. 44–53.

[2] See Tancred Borenius, 'The Rediscovery of the Primitives', *Quarterly Review* (Apr. 1923), pp. 268–9; Giovanni Previtali, *La Fortuna dei Primitivi*, Turin, 1964, pp. 176–80, 182–4.

prevailed in the wake of the French armies. The title-page of the sale catalogue of some of his drawings in 1804 frankly describes the contents as having been acquired 'during the revolutionary troubles in Italy, and the consequent pillage of the ancient Cabinets and Repositories there'.[1] Much of his time was devoted to art-historical researches. The greater part of the years 1792 and 1793, he told Dawson Turner,[2] was spent at Assisi, where he had the modern altar pieces removed in the Church of San Francesco, in order to make drawings of the frescoes of Giunta Pisano behind them, and sought diligently for manuscript records which might throw light on the frescoes of Cimabue and Giotto. In 1799 he returned home and settled in London, and Christie's held an important sale of forty-nine paintings from his collection in May 1801. In London he was a neighbour of T. F. Dibdin, and the latter claimed in his *Reminiscences* that he was the first 'to infect Ottley with the bibliomaniacal disease or mania—as it respected enquiries into the Origin of Printing',[3] a piece of research not printed until 1863, and its value limited by the fact that Ottley was a confirmed Haarlemite. Dibdin also, with characteristic circumlocution, referred to Ottley's interest in miniatures. 'My friend', he wrote, 'very soon and very successfully gave proof that the treasures of ancient art, scattered in the character of illuminations, through myriads of volumes in the British Museum, had attractions which might be instrumental to public instruction'; and Dibdin cited in evidence Ottley's long article in *Archaeologia*[4] on Harleian MS. 647, the famous Aratus in the British Museum, with astronomical illustrations derived from antique art. In his prefatory paragraph to that article, however, Ottley remarks that he had spent much of the four years before 1832 looking at fifteenth-century miniatures, in particular at the costumes depicted in them, with a view to their aid in dating block-books, which he was studying intensively. This takes us back to the antiquarian world of Strutt and his generation, but there is plenty of evidence that Ottley also studied miniatures as works of art.

[1] Gere, art. cit., p. 48.

[2] In a letter dated 2 Oct. 1826 (Trinity College, Cambridge, O. 13. 31[114]).

[3] *Reminiscences*, ii, 1836, p. 778.

[4] xxvi (1836), pp. 47–214.

When in 1817 Dibdin came to treat of 'Choral or Church-Service Books' in the first day of his *Bibliographical Decameron*, he introduced a footnote on this subject. 'My friend Mr. Ottley', he wrote, 'absolutely revels in the possession of the most splendid ancient fragments of books of this description, obtained by him, in Italy, from monasteries or private individuals. As no *names* are here mentioned, this general observation will be perfectly *stingless*.'[1] This must, I think, be an oblique reference to the purchase by Ottley in 1799 of a large group of drawings which had been stolen from a rival collector, J. B. J. Wicar. 'The copper-plates which belong to this portion of the *Bibliographical Decameron*', Dibdin continued, 'bear evidence of the wealth of my friend's collection—yet that collection, "rich and rare" as it is, was once of still greater extent.' The two plates of large initials, containing miniatures, from Ottley's collection includes one ascribed to the thirteenth century. 'One "great and glorious" sample of ancient art, exhibited in Choral Books', reported Dibdin, 'Mr. Ottley, however, still possesses; which must unquestionably be considered as the *Jupiter planet* of the system. In other words, it was executed by the famous Don Silvestro degli Angeli, and is described by Vasari as the chef-d'œuvre both of the artist and of the age.' Dibdin then goes on to describe in detail Ottley's large miniature of the Death of the Virgin,[2] and in a long note later in the volume he gives some account of Franco Bolognese and Don Silvestro, derived from Vasari and Baldinucci. I cannot resist quoting Dibdin's conclusion to this account, written in his most absurd vein. 'Where rest now', mused the Doctor, 'the ("pickled" is a most odious and unsavory expression!) embalmed "right hands" of these book-adorning monastic brothers? I own I should prefer them, in my cabinet, to the choicest mummy that ever had its perpendicular resting place against the walls of the most magnificent Aegyptian catacomb.'[3]

Dibdin refers to a group of illuminated Choir Books which had been sold at Sotheby's on 1 May 1816, books, he said, 'of a bulk and breadth that forbade ordinary shoulders to bear them away'.

1 *Bibliographical Decameron*, i, 1817, p. cxi.

2 Subsequently lot 181 in Ottley's sale of 11 May 1838, and thence, via the collections of the Revd. J. Fuller Russell and George Salting, to the British Museum, Add. MS. 37955A.

3 *Bibliographical Decameron*, i, 1817, p. cxxvi.

Certainly their size alone was an element in their frequent dismemberment. Another factor, which I have not seen cited, must also have been a powerful inducement to vandalism. On bound manuscripts and on books printed before 1801 there was an import duty of £6. 10*s*. 0*d*. per hundredweight.[1] Small wonder, therefore, that a dealer who had bought in Italy half a dozen elephant-folio Antiphonals was tempted to jettison the bindings and unilluminated pages and bring home only the decorative and saleable initials. One of the most important sales of such material ever to be held took place at Christie's on 26 May 1825 (see line illust. p. 66), when there was dispersed 'a highly valuable and extremely curious collection of illumined miniature paintings, of the greatest beauty, and of exquisite finishing, taken from the Choral Books of the Papal Chapel in the Vatican, during the French Revolution; and subsequently collected and brought to this country by the Abate Celotti'. I have had occasion to refer to the importations of this great dealer in my *Phillipps Studies*;[2] in 1825 he was exceptionally active, and apart from the sale in question consignments of books and manuscripts were included in three sales at Sotheby's in the same year, totalling nearly 4,000 lots. Ottley drew up the sale catalogue of the miniatures for Christie, and with its learned Introduction, elaborate descriptions, historical notes, and occasional attributions to specific artists, the cataloguing was of a standard hitherto entirely unknown.

Ottley draws attention in his Introduction to the paucity of information about the artists of this period, and provides a justification for their study.

> It is to be regretted [he wrote] that we possess but very incomplete accounts of those Artists of the thirteenth and following centuries, to whom we are indebted for the laborious, and often splendid performances, which decorate the Choral Books and other Manuscripts written in Italy during those periods. Sometimes, it is true, these Illuminations were the work of Monks and Nuns, or other religious persons, who, being insufficiently instructed in design, could do little more than evince their devotion to their patron saints by the prodigal use of gold and fine colours. Still, it is certain that the leisure of a cloister often produced

[1] *Phillipps Studies*, iii, 1954, pp. 33–5.

[2] Ibid., p. 50.

A

CATALOGUE

OF A

HIGHLY VALUABLE AND EXTREMELY CURIOUS COLLECTION OF

ILLUMINED MINIATURE PAINTINGS,

OF THE GREATEST BEAUTY, AND OF EXQUISITE FINISHING,

Taken from the Choral Books of the Papal Chapel in the Vatican, during the French Revolution; and subsequently collected and brought to this Country by the

ABATE CELOTTI.

The above Collection is highly important for the illustration of the Art of Painting in Italy during the fifteenth and following centuries; exhibiting, besides many fine productions of the Miniaturists, whose names have not been preserved by any Biographer, presumed specimens of the early masters, Francesco Squarcione and Giovanni Bellini; and undoubted chef d'œuvres of Girolamo de' Libri, and his disciple Giulio Clovio, who brought the Art to the highest perfection, as also by some other great Painters who lived after Clovio's time. The whole are described in a Catalogue, drawn in Chronological series by a gentleman well conversant in the History of early Italian Art.

WHICH

Will be Sold by Auction,

BY MR. CHRISTIE,

AT HIS GREAT ROOM,

NO. 8, KING STREET, ST. JAMES'S SQUARE,

On THURSDAY, MAY 26th, 1825,

AT ONE PRECISELY.

May be Viewed two days preceding, and Catalogues had (at One Shilling each) of Mr. Christie, 8, *King Street, St. James's Square.*

Artists of great ability in this way; and, besides these, Italy has been at all times provided with schools of professed Illuminists or Miniature Painters, of a superior order; whose works are alike estimable for their beauty and interesting as examples, showing generally, though upon a small scale, the style of Art that prevailed at the times, and in the schools, in which they were done: and these specimens are, in many cases, found in a more perfect state of preservation than the frescoes and other large works of painting remaining to us of the same periods. To this it may be added, that the processes which were resorted to by the ancient Illuminists, in preparing and laying on the different metals used in decorating their paintings, and in mixing their colours, have long ceased to be remembered; so that whatever performances of this kind now remain to us, merit also our regard as the *monuments of a lost Art.*[1]

Ottley then goes on to list, from various sources, those early artists, who, in his phrase, 'occasionally condescended to paint in miniature'—Giotto, Simone Martini, Fra Angelico, Don Bartolomeo della Gatta, and Cosimo Tura of Ferrara—and he cites, of course, two names famous from having been recorded in Dante and thence in Vasari, Oderigo da Gubbio and Franco Bolognese. We have certainly moved a long way in a short time from the era of Strutt and Sir John Fenn.

The collection of miniatures catalogued in ninety-seven lots sold remarkably well. A group of the miniatures has been recently studied by Professor Julian Brown,[2] who has identified the probable source of a series of cuttings as Sistine Chapel MS. A. I. 17, a Lectionary written for Pope Gregory XIII. Students of bibliophily will find several unfamiliar names among the buyers at this sale. Ottley himself bought heavily, but not in his own name. Samuel Rogers attended and bought several lots in person. The picture dealers also competed, and this was a relatively new development, although in 1817 Dibdin recorded that Samuel Woodburn had some miniatures from manuscripts in stock.[3]

Ottley collected miniatures and illuminations all his life, and after his death these were dispersed by Sotheby on 11–12 May 1838,

[1] *Catalogue*, Christie, 26 May 1825, p. 3.

[2] *British Museum Quarterly*, xxiii, No. 1 (1960), pp. 2–5.

[3] *Bibliographical Decameron*, i, 1817, p. cxii.

probably the most important sale of such material ever to be held, and one from which many of the finest items in the cabinets of other great collectors, such as Samuel Rogers, R. S. Holford, and Lord Northwick, were derived. In the sale there is evidence suggesting that Ottley himself dismembered manuscripts. Lot 127 consisted of twenty miniatures 'by an unknown French artist of the thirteenth or fourteenth century . . . most splendidly gilt and coloured'. Madden's sharp eye observed that these had been removed from lot 244, *Psalterium Davidicum*, and at his recommendation the two lots were sold together, being bought in for £37. 10*s*. 0*d*., and sold subsequently to Payne and Foss, who resold the item to R. S. Holford. At this date the detached miniatures were again inserted and the volume bound in red velvet by Lewis. It was not, however, until after the purchase of the volume by the Pierpont Morgan Library in 1927 that the late Dr. E. G. Millar did the jigsaw puzzle properly, and the book was again rebound in its correct order. It is now known to the world as Morgan MS. 729, the Psalter and Hours, written about 1290, probably at Amiens, for Yolande, Vicomtesse de Soissons, one of the acknowledged masterpieces of French Gothic illumination.

We shall have more to say about the fate of some of Ottley's miniatures when we refer to R. S. Holford's collection in our final chapter. Chronologically, we have, at Ottley's death, got some way ahead of the period now under review; and we must revert to the consideration of an earlier collector, also influential in our theme.

William Roscoe (1753–1831), the Liverpool historian, is of prime importance as an early collector of Italian primitives,[1] among which he included miniatures cut from manuscripts (Plate 10). He dealt with Ottley: the large initial with a miniature of the Birth of St. John by Don Silvestro Camaldolese, now in the Walker Art Gallery, came, for example, from Ottley's collection. Roscoe's chapter on the Arts in his *Life of Lorenzo de' Medici*, published in 1796, reflects the taste of his day, and the current view of the middle ages as a long

[1] See Michael Compton, 'William Roscoe and Early Collectors of Italian Primitives' *Liverpool Bulletin*, Walker Art Gallery Number, ix (1960–1), pp. 27–51.

night in which could be discerned dimly the streaks of the dawn of the Renaissance.

> The crude buds [he wrote] that had escaped the severity of so long a winter, soon began to swell, and Giotto, Buffalmacco, and Gaddi, were the contemporaries of Dante, of Boccaccio and of Petrarca.
>
> It was not, however, to be presumed, that even in the darkest intervals of the middle ages, these arts were entirely extinguished. . . . Among the manuscripts of the Laurentian library, are preserved some specimens of miniature painting which are unquestionably to be referred to the tenth century, but they bear decisive evidence of the barbarism of the times; and although they certainly aim at picturesque representation, yet they may with justice be considered rather as perverse distortions of nature, than as the commencement of an elegant art.[1]

The failure of Roscoe's bank and the enforced sale of his library and other collections in 1816 are well known. These had been partly assembled with a view to writing an 'Historical sketch of the State of the Arts in the Middle Ages', a project which was abandoned. Instead, in his retirement, Roscoe undertook the preparation of a catalogue of the famous collection of manuscripts at Holkham, the inherited property of his friend and patron Thomas Coke, enriched by a few but very important accessions made by Coke himself. The sad and complicated story of Roscoe's catalogue, its revision by Madden, Dawson Turner's involvement in the preparation of its plates, and the final abandonment by Coke of its publication has been well told by Mrs. J. E. Graham.[2] To her I am indebted for drawing my attention to a draft of an unpublished essay by Roscoe compiled in connection with the Holkham catalogue, in which he sketches the history of medieval book illumination in Italy.[3] The essay was attached to the description of a richly decorated Bible, described by Dorez as 'one of the most beautiful books executed in the first half of the XIVth century, belonging perhaps to the Anti-Pope Clement VII'.[4] This had previously belonged to Roscoe

[1] *Life of Lorenzo de' Medici*, ii, 1796, pp. 175–6.

[2] Mrs. J. E. Graham, 'The Cataloguing of the Holkham Manuscripts', *Transactions of the Cambridge Bibliographical Society*, iv, Pt. 2 (1965), pp. 128–54.

[3] Liverpool Public Library, Roscoe MS. 5551.

[4] B.M. Add. MS. 47672: Léon Dorez, *Les Manuscrits à peintures de la bibliothèque de Lord Leicester*, Paris, 1908, p. 44.

himself and Coke bid for it at the sale in 1816. Two Liverpool booksellers bought it for £178, but Roscoe induced them to pass it on to Coke for 200 guineas.

In his description of the manuscript Roscoe quotes a letter from Ottley written on 11 November 1813, which shows that the latter had it in his possession for some weeks and had shown it to several other connoisseurs. On the miniatures Ottley ventures a precise opinion.

> From their peculiar character [he wrote] I am persuaded that they were executed by an Italian artist in the School of Giotto, in the beginning of the XIVth century. Giotto was employed for a considerable time at Avignon under Clement V, who first transferred the papal chair from Rome to France in 1305, and it is very probable that this Bible may have been written in France soon after that time and adorned with miniatures, as I have said, executed in the School of Giotto.

Roscoe's attached essay runs to some nineteen pages, and must be one of the fullest accounts of the subject written in English at this date. It is, indeed, not particularly profound or original (Roscoe never visited Italy), but it brings together a good deal of information from Vasari, Baldinucci, Lanzi, and other sources. We start, of course, with the famous passage in Dante, and from Oderico we pass, via Cimabue, Giotto, and Don Silvestro, to the frontispiece of Petrarch's Vergil painted by Simone Martini, and thence, via Cosimo Tura, Francesco, and Girolamo dai Libri, to Giulio Clovio, with whom, says Roscoe, 'the history of illuminating books seems to close'. Roscoe's view of Clovio is of course the traditional one of his period. 'By his extraordinary genius and exquisite performances', he concluded, '[Clovio] has given to the miniature a rank and dignity scarcely to be exceeded by any department of the art.'

If Roscoe's connoisseurship was, in Mr. Compton's phrase, 'not much better than the standards of his time',[1] he did at all events see point in acquiring manuscripts unfashionable in his day, but which have subsequently been hailed as masterpieces of Gothic art. It was he who supplied Coke with one of the most famous of all the

[1] Op. cit., p. 47.

Holkham manuscripts, the Bible Picture Book,[1] an English work of the early fourteenth century, reproduced in 1954 in a lavish facsimile by Dr. W. O. Hassall. Roscoe regarded it 'as a preparation for a Block-book and . . . one of the greatest curiosities I ever saw'. It had been offered to him by Winstanley, the Liverpool auctioneer, for £30, and Roscoe offered it to Coke at this price, 'if you should take a liking to such a dislocated set of figures on account of their antiquity'. Seldom can thirty pounds have been better spent.

Coke also, in 1818, bought four noble manuscripts looted from the monastery of Weingarten by General Thiébaul tin 1806, which were subsequently consigned by the Parisian dealer Delahante to Phillips, the London auctioneer, who offered them to Coke at £200. Since three were in medieval jewelled bindings, and one was the Anglo-Saxon Gospels given to Weingarten by the Lady Judith, daughter of Baldwin, Earl of Flanders, this does not seem an extravagant figure, but some hard bargaining reduced it to 100 guineas. From our point of view two letters of Francis Douce add interest to the episode. He was asked to advise on the desirability of the acquisition, and this he urged, but purely for the sake of the bindings. 'MSS. with such covers are extremely rare everywhere,' he wrote, 'nor do I remember to have seen any in this country. They have not more than 8 or 10 in the Royal Library at Paris . . . The paintings are rude and of little value as being of common subjects.' So much for the Winchester School and its appreciation in 1818 by one of the most acute connoisseurs of his day. The unpublished Roscoe–Madden catalogue of the Holkham manuscripts,[2] when it deals with this group of Weingarten books, provides a long essay on medieval jewelled bindings, certainly the fullest account of the subject written in English at that date. The four manuscripts are now in the Pierpont Morgan Library.[3]

We must now consider Dibdin's opening chapter of *The Bibliographical Decameron*, in which he seeks to give 'a strict view of the

[1] B.M. Add. MS. 47682.

[2] Still at Holkham. I have used the fair copy given by Coke to Lord Brougham, vols. i and iv of which are in the library of the Grolier Club, New York.

[3] Pierpont Morgan MSS. 708–11.

progress of the Arts of Design and Composition, in illuminated MSS. from the Vth to the XVIth century inclusive'. It runs to more than 200 pages, with over sixty illustrations, including fourteen full-page plates, and as the earliest extensive and influential account of the subject for the 'general reader', it must be taken seriously. My affection for Dibdin is great, but it is hard taxed by this section of his work. It is not so much the facetiousness and absurdities which make difficult the extraction of hard facts, as the arrangement, which, in a work devoted to 'a strict view of the progress of the arts', a naïve reader, not knowing his Dibdin, might expect to be chronological. Instead, the Doctor deals with his theme by subjects—Bibles, Missals, Heraldry, Chronicles, Romances, and so on—and only by performing a major task of tabulation is it possible to gather together what he records on, say, this tenth-century illumination. A specimen of the material from which information has to be quarried will not come amiss at this point.

LYSANDER. We will pass on, if you please, to the Order of the Day. Shall *Missals* be the first note to touch, in your approaching calligraphical concert?

PHILEMON. 'Missals'—with all my heart. Yet, as a volume of *anterior* execution, and as partaking in some degree of the warblings of the muse, pray let me introduce to your especial notice a vastly pretty group of females—from a ponderous tome of the works of CHRISTINE DE PISA, in the British Museum. I observe that the Ladies are absolutely envious of the *head-dresses* of their sex at the commencement of the *Fifteenth Century*! Allow, at any rate, that the grouping and its accessories are pretty and interesting.[1]

As a method of introducing a facsimile of a miniature, and, in a long footnote, a description of Harleian MS. 4431, this seems rather circuitous. Dibdin, however, rated the miniature highly, describing it as 'really not unworthy of some of the happier efforts of Stothard'. Nevertheless, Dibdin does draw attention to many manuscripts never described in print before, and he is also a source of information on many collectors who would otherwise be mere names in the British Museum's *List of Catalogues of English Book Sales*. Dibdin

[1] *Bibliographical Decameron*, i, 1817, p. cxxxiv.

begins by taking issue with the 'scurrilous, saucy, but not unsagacious' Abbé Rive, who had the 'hardihood or ignorance' to describe illumination between the tenth and the mid fourteenth centuries as almost entirely frightful: in *his* work Dibdin adds, he hopes to teach a different lesson.

Of the earliest books he gives a fair coverage. We start, of course, with books which Dibdin had never seen—their descriptions derived from Montfaucon, Bandini, and other palaeographers—the Vatican Vergil and Terence, the Ambrosian Homer, the Vienna Genesis. On the Lindisfarne Gospels Dibdin is rapturous, 'the proudest bibliomaniacal monument of the earlier period of our history'. 'The Athelstan-book of the Gospels'[1] is, on the other hand, 'dismally barbarous in the ornamental part: I fear the female part of my audience would not scruple to express their suprise, or even loathing, at the sight of those apple-green and smoke-dried old figures intended to represent the Evangelists.' The Stowe Missal, now in the Royal Irish Academy, and St. Chad's Gospels at Lichfield are commended, and so is a Psalter of which Dibdin gives a reproduction.[2] The Hyde Abbey Book,[3] then also at Stowe, and the Bodleian Cædmon provide illustrations; and the Benedictional of St. Æthelwold is rightly singled out as being 'among our chief treasures of specimens of ancient art'. The miniatures are listed, and bear such brief comments as 'strikingly splendid', 'very tasteful', and so on—'a very harvest-field for the antiquary to disport himself in'.

A section on the earliest Greek manuscripts follows, with some rapturous remarks on *codices purpurei*, and among the plates is reproduced the miniature of St. Luke from a copy of the Gospels in the library of John Dent.[4] With regard to manuscripts from the twelfth to the early fourteenth centuries it is interesting to determine exactly what Dibdin had himself seen; clearly it is comparatively little. His examples are drawn almost exclusively from the British Museum, the Bodleian, and a few other collections in London and Oxford. He cites the twelfth-century Florence of Worcester at Corpus Christi College, Oxford, and reproduces some line-drawings from it from

[1] B.M. MS. Cott. Tiberius A. II.

[2] B.M. MS. Cott. Titus D. XXVII.

[3] B.M. MS. Stowe 944.

[4] Pierpont Morgan MS. 639.

tracings supplied by Henry Petrie, who also provided notes on two or three manuscripts in the Public Library at Rouen. He draws attention to the splendidly decorated Life and Miracles of St. Edmund,[1] which he had seen in the auction room when John Towneley's library was sold by Evans in 1814. He reproduces further twelfth-century initials from the glossed Epistles of St. Paul at Christ Church, Oxford, and invites the reader to admire 'the graceful flow of lines, in spite of the singularity' of the illustration. Dibdin had a genuine feeling for decoration of this date, which, he said, displays 'perfect taste in the arabesque, with occasionally much successful union of the droll and fantastical'. Among books of this period, Dibdin also knew, and reproduced an initial from, the Chronicle of Abingdon.[2]

It was to be expected that Dibdin's love of the quaint and the grotesque would lead him to enthuse over Bestiaries. 'Walk in Ladies and Gentlemen, and you shall see the Lions and a thousand four-footed oddities.' Such is his introduction to St. John's College, Oxford, MS. LXI and Bodleian, Ashmole 1511. In his description of the latter manuscript, among much zoological chit-chat, are some sound artistic judgements. The miniaturist is commended for his skill in design, the nicety of his finish, and the dexterity with which he had applied his gold leaf. The style of art, he avers, is 'in no way contemptible, but on the contrary has great pretensions to elegance and accuracy'. This, for its date, is quite an advanced view of twelfth-century painting.

On Psalters Dibdin is superficial and perfunctory. Queen Mary's Psalter is accorded a long description and the outline drawings granted great merit.[3] The illuminations in the text, however, are dismissed as being 'almost uniformly clumsy and unsuccessful'. Bodleian Gough 194 and Royal Society MSS. 60 and 155 are the only other Psalters to which he refers, and he had obviously not seen the grandest examples of this class of book, which represents the peak of English Gothic book-painting. The fourteenth-century manuscript which aroused Dibdin's greatest enthusiasm was the

[1] Pierpont Morgan MS. 736.
[2] B.M. MS. Cott. Claudius B. VI.
[3] B.M. MS. Royal 2 B. VII.

'Roman d'Alexandre' at Oxford,[1] the 'Jupiter Romaunt-Planet of the Bodleian Library'.

> Let the day be ever so dark—let the wind blow ever so coldly through the crevices of the mullions, or of the panes of glass, in that vast book-repository—you have here a luminary, whose rays, darting upwards, (like the light in Correggio's famous *Notte*) equally diffuse light and heat. These rays animated Tom Warton, and they even warmed John Price: and certainly, in one of the coldest of the early November days, these same rays caused the writer of this most strange note to glow as if the thermometer were at 72 in a northern aspect![2]

Strutt had already drawn lavishly upon this book for his illustrations; Dibdin therefore contents himself with the reproduction of four drawings only.

Book-painting up to the mid fourteenth century occupies only perhaps an eighth of Dibdin's opening chapter. The remaining 200 pages are devoted to descriptions of later books famous in their day, and a few of them, the Bedford Missal, for example, famous still. The greatest space given to any manuscript is the thirteen pages describing the Missal of Cardinal Della Rovere, to which we have referred. Several manuscripts which had come on to the market at the recent sale of James Edwards's library are singled out, the Hours, for example, of Ferdinand I, King of Naples,[3] for which Dibdin himself paid £125, and, after having had a plate engraved from it for his book, passed it on to the Marquis of Douglas for the same sum. Another showy book bought at the Edwards sale and used for an illustration was 'Les Chroniques des Gestes du Roy Françoys I',[4] which Dibdin then transferred to the library of his friend John North. The Missal of Henry VII at Chatsworth is commended as 'very curious and lovely' and the floral borders inspire a quotation from Thomson's *Autumn*. Yet another was the 'Roman Breviary possessed by Mr. Dent', described in a footnote of some 2,000 words.

[1] MS. Bodley 264.

[2] *Bibliographical Decameron*, i, 1817, p. cxcviii.

[3] Berlin, Kupferstichkabinett 78 D 14.

[4] Destroyed. See Louis Paris, *Les mss. de la Bibliothèque du Louvre brûlés dans la nuit du 23 au 24 mai 1871 sous le règne de la Commune*, Paris, 1872, p. 65, No. 336. I owe this note to the kindness of M. François Avril of the Bibliothèque Nationale.

This manuscript, executed for Queen Isabella of Spain with a (hitherto) blank leaf adorned with a miniature of St. Catherine, passed, on Dibdin's advice, to Sir John Tobin, and thence to the British Museum.[1] There is a long account, and a plate of a sixteenth-century Flemish missal which had been hawked around the trade for some years, in the course of which its original stamped binding was replaced by modern green velvet, an act which aroused Dibdin's indignation. 'Such a proceeding was little short of rank barbarism,' he protested, 'and it is said that mister Charles Lewis, on receiving instructions to perform the operation, started backwards "three paces and mo"—while "the lights" in his workshop "burnt blue"!!' There are references to other late missals in the collections of Henry Broadley,[2] of Ferriby, near Hull, and of Sir Mark Masterman Sykes; and to the Lamoignon Missal in the great library of Thomas Johnes of Hafod, a collector previously cited as the owner of an especially sumptuous copy of 'L'Arbre des Battailles', who also reappears, in the final section of this chapter, among the owners of splendid romances of chivalry, along with the Duke of Devonshire, Robert Lang,[3] and E. V. Utterson.[4]

In his *Northern Tour*[5] Dibdin records a visit to John Trotter Brockett of Newcastle (1788–1842). In 1818 this lawyer and antiquary had initiated the Typographical Society of Newcastle, which had produced a series of privately printed tracts. A large part of this collector's library, especially rich in books on coins and medals, was dispersed by Sotheby in a sale which began on 8 December 1823; and the residue came under the hammer in 1843 after his death. This relatively modest provincial collector would not qualify for a place in these pages, had not a happy chance brought on to my own

[1] B.M. Add. MS. 18851.

[2] Henry Broadley (1793–1851), M.P. for the East Riding, Yorks., 1837–51; his elder brother, John Broadley, F.S.A. (b. 1784), was a better-known collector. Evans held two sales of parts of his library, on 12 July 1832 and 19 June 1833; the first part contained a number of important illuminated manuscripts.

[3] Robert Lang, of Portland Place. Phillipps bought over twenty-five romances at his sale (17 Nov. 1823): see *Phillipps Studies*, iii, 1954, p. 55.

[4] Edward Vernon Utterson (? 1776–1856), Clerk in Chancery, mainly a collector and editor of early English poetry, original member of the Roxburghe Club 1812.

[5] *A Bibliographical Antiquarian and Picturesque Tour in the Northern Counties of England and Scotland*, i, 1838, pp. 390–3.

shelves an elaborate catalogue of his manuscripts, completed by Brockett on 5 October 1831. The title-page, in a variety of scripts against a background of crumbling masonry, has an agreeable period flavour. The manuscripts, about 120 in number, in part relate to the topography and history of Durham, and some of these are today among the Raine manuscripts in the Chapter library.[1] Twenty others, however, are medieval in date and include a number of decorated service books. The cataloguing is of an elaboration rare at this period and includes pen-facsimiles of scripts and copies of miniatures. Brockett's enthusiasm for his task seems to have fluctuated as he proceeded, but he was still able to devote five folio pages to his description of MS. LXI, a Roman Pontifical, with an index of the contents and emblazoned drawings of five coats-of-arms which appear in the manuscript. The descriptions are perhaps better evidence of Brockett's love of his manuscripts than of his scholarship: nevertheless, he deserves an entry when some new De Ricci rewrites the history of bibliophily.

At this point we ought to consider a handful of collectors of medieval manuscripts of the period who do not feature largely in Dibdin's Temple of Fame. Foremost among them was William Beckford, a lone wolf among collectors and outside the close little coterie of the Roxburghe Club circle. Few books are more eagerly awaited than Mr. Anthony Hobson's study of Beckford as a connoisseur, the preparation of which has been deferred, but not, it is much to be hoped, *sine die*. Ten years ago he whetted our appetite in a paper read to the Bibliographical Society, and with characteristic generosity he has lent me the unpublished typescript, from which the following remarks are derived.

Beckford attended the La Vallière sale of 1784 in person and bought two manuscript Books of Hours. He shared his contemporaries' predilection for books which were late, and was attracted to the Roman rather than the Gothic script, hence his ownership of some fine Italian humanistic manuscripts and sixteenth-century *Officia B.V.M.* In 1803 he was to be found in Paris buying a manuscrip by Jarry at the Dusquenoy sale.

[1] I am indebted to Dr. A. I. Doyle for this information.

His judgment of quality, however [wrote Mr. Hobson], matured progressively. Of his first purchase, at the La Vallière sale, he wrote that it was 'glittering with gold letters and curious miniatures—where among other nonsensical figures shine Juppiter and Juno married by a Gothic priest before the image of our Redeemer'. By 1832, however, he was observing to his bookseller, George Clarke, that 'the style and execution of the miniatures is the principal object', and in the last two years of his life he bought the Hours of Mary of Burgundy,[1] the finest manuscript in his collection.

This had previously belonged to Philip Augustus Hanrott, at the five sales of whose library, held in 1833 to 1834, Beckford bought heavily. De Ricci remarks upon the paucity of information about Hanrott, and in this context it is worth quoting from a newspaper cutting inserted in Dawson Turner's copy of the sale catalogues.[2]

Great legal failure of the firm of Hanrott and Metcalfe . . . [which] has created the greatest consternation . . . The partners were universally respected . . . The partnership has since the event been dissolved; and we have seen a letter of Mr. M's in which he acquits himself of all knowledge or participation in the defalcations of his partner. Mr. Philip Augustus Hanrott was a literary as well as a legal man; his library being considered an unusually rich one; his habits being altogether of a refined character, his present misfortune is the more unaccountable.

This suggests that the sale may not have been a voluntary one. Some years ago I bought two (of four) volumes of Hanrott's own manuscript catalogue of his library, drawn up between 1828 and 1831. There are a few early manuscripts, a twelfth-century St. Isidore of Seville, for example, and a thirteenth-century Bede 'with some curious illuminations'. The majority, however, are late humanistic or liturgical books, against some of which Hanrott has recorded his comments. 'Curious as a specimen of art', he noted against a fifteenth-century Roman missal. Hanrott owned some fine things, among them the dismembered Carmelite Missal so ably reconstructed by Dr. Margaret Rickert,[3] and also the enchanting fifteenth-century Greek

[1] Berlin, Kupferstichkabinett 78 B 12.

[2] Harvard, Houghton Library, W. A. Jackson Collection.

[3] B.M. Add. MSS. 29704–5, 44892: see Margaret Rickert, *The Reconstructed Carmelite Missal*, 1952.

manuscript of Aesop,[1] written in Italy and decorated with 131 miniatures, secured at this sale by Sir Thomas Phillipps. It is, however, characteristic of the age that the most famous of all his books was his printed vellum copy of the *Sforziada*, Milan, 1490, with its superb decoration, miniature portraits and contemporary velvet binding adorned with silver *nielli*. This had a noble provenance—the Prince de Soubise, Count MacCarthy, and George Hibbert, the banker. Dibdin saw it in the library of the last-named and waxed rapturous. 'We have here the loveliest—or at any rate, and without question or doubt ONE of the loveliest—of membranaceous bijoux!' This passed into the hands of another old-fashioned collector, Thomas Grenville, and then to the British Museum.

An earlier and discriminating connoisseur whose manuscripts can be studied in their entirety was Richard, Viscount Fitzwilliam, who in 1816 bequeathed to Cambridge University among his collections 130 manuscripts of which 104 were acquired between 1808 and 1815. No less than ninety-seven of them were Books of Hours of the late fifteenth and very early sixteenth centuries, the largest group of such books, I believe, assembled by any collector of that period. Lord Fitzwilliam was unusual in so far as he acquired very few of the fashionable manuscripts of the mid sixteenth century and very few humanistic books. His *Horae* were of very varying quality, but included several of the first rank, No. 60 for example, the Hours of Jeanne Raguenel, written before 1418, and No. 62, the Hours of Isabella Stuart, with no less than 528 miniatures executed at the workshop of the Maître de Rohan. M. R. James also rated very highly the decoration of MS. No. 28, the Milanese Pontifical, written between 1433 and 1443. From our point of view perhaps his most interesting accession was MS. No. 12, the well-known Psalter written at Peterborough about 1220, rather an advanced purchase for such a collector to have made in 1807.

We mentioned above Sir Thomas Phillipps, who already by 1830 had acquired a large number of sumptuous illuminated manuscripts. A collector so omnivorous is difficult to call in evidence in any particular cause, but we may cite a few examples of such books, which

[1] New York Public Library, Spencer Collection, MS. 50.

he bought, so to speak, on purpose, rather than in one of his great drag-net operations, such as the Leander Van Ess purchase, or in the indiscriminate fury with which he beat down opposition at the Meerman sale. The best instance of Phillipps's exercising choice is to be found in the eight lots he bought at the auction of the library of the Revd. Theodore Williams in 1827. These included the superb Gospels of Mathilda of Tuscany,[1] the eleventh-century Gundulf Bible,[2] and the fifteenth-century Dictys Cretensis, with exquisite miniatures in *camaïeu-bleu*, which Mrs. Chester Beatty cajoled Phillipps's grandson into selling her in 1925:[3] nor were the other five lots by any means negligible. I must concur in Mr. A. E. Popham's judgement that Phillipps's artistic appreciation was nil,[4] but at all events he was no slavish follower of fashion.

In this chapter we must let Dibdin, the barometer of the taste of his period, have the final say. For me, perhaps the most typical example of contemporary standards of connoisseurship is to be found in the seven closely-printed pages[5] which he devotes to the twelve drawings of the Victories of Charles V in the collection of Thomas Grenville (Plate 11).[6] Dibdin's description of this once-renowned series derives from the notes appended to them by Grenville himself. The book had been looted by a French officer from the Escorial, and secured by the picture-dealer Woodburn from a Parisian colleague in the trade. Ottley, Douce, and Richard Payne Knight had all examined it and had attributed the paintings to the great Giulio Clovio himself. Later connoisseurs have been more cautious. J. W. Bradley in 1891 was disposed to award the Master at least one of the miniatures, but the greater part of his discussion of the series is devoted to the question of whether they were copied from Heemskerck's engravings of 1556 or from Heemskerck's drawings for his engravings.[7] In 1911 they score an entry of one line in J. A. Herbert's *Illuminated Manuscripts*, by that date relegated to a pupil or imitator of Clovio, who himself is condemned for 'his mawkish sentiment, want of dignity and florid taste'.

[1] Pierpont Morgan MS. 492.
[2] Henry E. Huntington Lib. MS. 62.
[3] *Phillipps Studies*, v, 1960, pp. 74–5: now Chester Beatty Library, Dublin, W. 122.
[4] Ibid. iv, 1956, p. 224.
[5] *Bibliographical Decameron*, i, 1817, pp. clxxxviii–cxciv.
[6] B.M. Add. MS. 33733.
[7] *The Life and Works of Giulio Clovio*, 1891, pp. 275–89.

Dibdin concludes the First Day of his *Bibliographical Decameron* with a rhetorical exhortation to the authorities of the British Museum to publish a series of facsimiles of illuminated manuscripts in the National Collection.

> I augur well [he wrote] from the known sagacity and invincible diligence of those gentlemen to whose care such a Repository is now confided, that very many years will not elapse before we receive some specimen, or specimens, in the way of *graphic illustration*, of the beautiful, curious, extraordinary, or instructive exhibitions of ancient art which that Repository contains. The wealth of a nation is never better bestowed than in the diffusion of useful or elegant knowledge, and least of all should *that* knowledge be suffered to lie concealed, which by calling forth, and embodying with new life, as it were, what our Ancestors have done, tends most effectually to perpetuate a meritorious remembrance of Ourselves—and what is this, let me ask, but Fame and Patriotism in their purest 'shapes and substances'?[1]

Colour-printing and photography led to a wider circulation of facsimiles of medieval miniatures throughout the nineteenth century, but, so far as any official publication was involved, Dibdin overrated the 'invincible diligence' of the officers of the Museum; and eighty years were to elapse before Sir George Warner's series of facsimiles of illuminated manuscripts was laid before the public.

[1] *Bibliographical Decameron*, i, 1817, p. ccxxiv.

V *Robert Curzon ⋄ friendship with Walter Sneyd ⋄ Parham ⋄ Philobiblon Society ⋄ his letters written from the Middle East ⋄* Visits to Monasteries in the Levant ⋄ Catalogue of Materials for Writing ⋄ *later accessions of manuscripts*

IN the third chapter I wrote at some length on a single collector, Francis Douce, whose quiet, austere, and formal life was not much leavened by humour, let alone hilarity. In sharp contrast I now invite the reader to share my delight when I investigated the collections and personalities of two collectors of the next generation, lifelong friends, both dedicated to their manuscripts and both characters of singular charm and humanity. They are Robert Curzon, author of *Visits to Monasteries in the Levant*, one of the best travel books in the language, and Walter Sneyd. The latter's collection is the more closely related to the narrow confines of this study; but the friends are indivisible and their friendship is marvellously documented. At Keele Hall, the ancestral home of the Sneyds and now part of the University of Keele, are preserved large portions of the family papers. These had passed into the possession of Mr. Raymond Richards, F.S.A., and were deposited by him in 1950 as part of a larger collection of antiquarian papers in the John Rylands Library. In 1957, however, Mr. Richards's collections were bought by the then University College of North Staffordshire and transferred to Keele, an exceptionally suitable place of deposit as many of them relate to the house and the estate. Among them are several catalogues and a group of letters relating to the Sneyd library. For me, however, there was a correspondence infinitely more rewarding: a series of no less than 506 letters from Curzon to Sneyd, covering a period of more than forty years.[1] In them Curzon writes without reservation to his

[1] These have been most admirably calendared for the National Register of Archives by the Archivist of Keele, Mr. Ian H. C. Fraser, to whose knowledge of the Sneyd family and Keele I am greatly indebted. Hereafter references to these letters carry Mr. Fraser's numeration.

oldest friend; they are full of wit, humour, and agreeable gossip about book-collecting in general and their own two collections in particular; and the pleasure they gave me must be my excuse for allowing Curzon in his *ipsissima verba* to usurp a considerable part of this chapter.

First let me recite briefly the outlines of the two friends' lives. Both were of aristocratic lineage. The Sneyds of Staffordshire numbered among their illustrious forebears a knight who distinguished himself at Poictiers, and a Warden of All Souls, while Curzon's mother was the Baroness de la Zouche in her own right, and his father the 2nd Viscount Curzon. Sneyd was born in 1809 and Curzon in 1810, and they were contemporaries at Christ Church, Oxford, where the bonds of their lifelong friendship were forged. Sneyd took his B.A. in 1831, whereas Curzon went down without a degree and was returned to Parliament for the family constituency of Clitheroe. In the House he conscientiously recorded his vote against every stage of the Reform Bill. On the disfranchisement of his seat in 1832 he cheerfully withdrew from politics for the rest of his life, and late in the same year he and Sneyd went off to Rome, where they passed the winter. Sneyd returned to England, took orders, and spent much of his life at Denton House, near Cuddesdon, in Oxfordshire, whereas Curzon began the series of travels with which his name will always be associated—in Egypt, the Holy Land, Albania, and Greece—exploring monastic libraries, many of them quite unknown at that date, and acquiring by purchase, barter, or gift some extraordinary manuscript treasures in the course of his visits. In 1841 he was appointed attaché at the embassy at Constantinople and private secretary to the ambassador, Sir Stratford Canning. Two years later he travelled into Armenia on a commission to arbitrate on the disputed boundary between Turkey and Persia, and became desperately ill with brain fever at Erzerum.

'I have been very nearly leaving you & the old books behind, O Sneyd', he wrote on 12 March 1843, '& that without making any will, so in case I should never get back to England I hereby bequeath all my manuscripts & books printed before 1525 to you, for your benefit and disport. However I hope it will please God to let me return safely some day, for none of my family are worthy of Parham, & the things contained in it, & I should like to brush it up, & carry into effect some of my schemes there before I die.'[1]

Parham, the beautiful Elizabethan house near Pulborough in Sussex, was Curzon's passion.[2] He filled it with armour and all sorts of Gothic *objets d'art*, 'gimcracks' as he always referred to them in his letters to Sneyd. His love for the house was intensified by the spendthrift and eccentric behaviour of his father, which stultified the splendid plans he had made for its upkeep and made its very retention precarious. The letters to Sneyd are full of sad complaints about his father, who never stopped treating his son as though he were a schoolboy and was full of odd habits and prejudices. 'He would give me the coat off his back, and then work himself up into a fury if I did not put in on in a way which pleased him', the son wrote in 1839. Curzon lived at Parham in his father's lifetime, but it was an uncomfortable existence; for while he worked hard with slender means to beautify and improve the estate, timber was intermittently being felled at his father's direction to satisfy the creditors. He came to dread his parents' visits, when the furniture with which he had lovingly adorned the rooms was brusquely rearranged. In 1858 total ruin overtook his father. 'My parents are coming here', the son wrote to Sneyd from Parham; 'they pay me a small sum to keep them. My Brother has got into another scrape & has more in prospect. The ruin which my father has so deliberately brought upon me has worried me into a fever.'[3] The old man did not die until 1863, leaving a perplexing tangle of debts behind him. If Curzon had not inherited £1,400 a year from an aunt's estate, Parham would have had to be sold.

In early life Curzon was often unhappy and lonely. It irked him that, having hardly the means to support himself in idleness, he had been trained to no profession. Endless travelling was his anodyne, not only abroad, but also at home, where he moved from one great

[1] Fraser No. 106.

[2] See *Parham in Sussex, A Historical and Descriptive Survey*, [by James Wentworth-Fitzwilliam], fol., privately printed, 1947. I am most grateful to the Hon. Mrs. Clive Pearson for hospitality at Parham and for help in several matters relating to the house and Robert Curzon.

[3] Fraser No. 279.

house of his aristocratic friends to another, Hagley, his father's residence, Arundel, Tabley, Castle Ashby, Up Park, and Fryston. 'Little snug old Denton' saw much of him; visits there were eagerly anticipated.

> Nobody here cares a bit for old Mss. or Oriental adventures [he wrote to Sneyd from Hagley in 1835]. So I dream to myself all day of the glorious things I have seen and hope to see some day or other & think how nice it must have been in the 15th century to wear a murrey coloured gown & read Sir Tristan de Leonois seated on a carved throne in an old Gothic room with the sun streaming on the illuminated pages of the book through the rare ymagerie of the mullioned window. Can't you fancy it, with a horn at the end of your toe half a foot long and the trees all burgeoning and the birds carolling outside, whereas now we [have] only new novels to read and the trees grow but I never saw one regularly burgeon in my life, and as for the carolling of birds one hears nothing but the twittering of sparrows all the year round; but when I come and stay with you, we will go back a century or two and ride Palfreys and Destruers in spite of the people calling them by the vulgar modern names of poneys and hacks, & if you would read one of my sermons by Erasmus or Melancthon I am certain that I should feel better for it, whatever the rest of the Congregation may do, and the clerk would have a sounder nap which would be a great thing for the old man . . .[1]

Curzon indeed induced his father to offer Sneyd the living of Wiggonholt near Parham, and assured him of a warm welcome if he would move to Sussex, but without success. 'We should have nothing to do', he wrote, 'but to take shady walks in the north Park between fowl, & Venison, & tomes & tomes, till we were laid by the side of each other in the little church at Parham.'

Both friends married rather late, Curzon in 1850 and Sneyd in 1856. Their marriages brought them great happiness, and Curzon was desolated by the death of his wife in 1866. In 1870 a change of status befell them both. Curzon, on the death of his mother, became the 14th Baron Zouche, an honour that gave him little pleasure. 'I am in a false position; my expenses are too great for my fortune, and I feel humbled & mortified because I cannot do what is expected

[1] Fraser No. 31.

of me', he wrote to his friend. In the same year Sneyd's elder brother died and he inherited the family estate at Keele, moving from Denton to the great new Salvin house, arranging his precious books in his brother's elaborately decorated library, and hastening to offer Curzon an interest-free loan, which the latter gratefully declined.

There is a most charming description of Parham at the end of Curzon's life by the Hon. Margaret Leicester Warren, who visited the house as a girl.[1]

> We got out into a square courtyard [she recorded on 28 January 1871], and walked up some steps into a grand old hall, hung round with armour, & then into a drawing room where was Lord Zouche, who was very kind and gave us tea and took us up to our rooms. I went to sleep that night in a wonderful bed: the top ceiling and curtains were made of red & white silk & lovely old Italian lace, & the framework part was all red velvet & gold. No doubt there were many ghosts in my room, for it was very large and solemn; the dressing table was like an altar in a chapel hung with lace & lighted with great silver candlesticks. Dim old portraits hung around; the one over the chimneypiece was of a lady dressed in faded cream colour, resting in a wood, with her hand on the neck of a pink dog; her lap full of flowers, & a crescent in her hair to show she had been hunting . . .

The isolation and the quiet of the house made a deep impression on the girl.

> Not even a neighbour ever seems to come here [she continued]. The great wood-fire burns in the hall & the great clock ticks, & the whole house is half asleep in the snow. Lord Zouche is very quiet & sad: he says 'his heart is broken & there is no joy in him'; he lives here quite alone with his little daughter Darea and her governess. The rest of the house is empty. After breakfast Lord Zouche took us over the house. The dining room looks far out on the wolds & fir woods. He showed us his museum and his own room, full of beautiful and wonderful things: old pictures & Albert Durer prints, first editions of Shakespeare & the Bible: gems and thumb-screws: Hebrew scrolls: 'alabaster boxes of ointment very precious': locks of King Charles' hair and armour of every country.

[1] Quoted in *Parham in Sussex* from her *Diaries*, 2 vols., privately printed, Taunton, 1924.

1. The Bedford Hours: portrait of the Duke. (*See p.* 3)

British Museum, Add. MS. 18850, f. 256^{v}

2. Copy made for the Abbé Rive of a seventeenth-century miniature of St. Nicholas in the style of Jarry added for Louis XIV to *B.M. Add. MS. 18553*, a Book of Hours executed for Francis I. (*See p.* 18)

British Museum, Add. MS. 15301, f. 50

3. Guyart Desmoulins, Bible historiale, early XIVth century, with miniatures described by a cataloguer in 1789 as being 'in the coarse manner of that age'. (*See p.* 22)

Bodleian Library, MS. Douce 211, f. 59^v

Dont en mena moy-
ses ysrael de la rou-
ge mer el desert de
sur Glosa De sur li
Ebrieu ethamnes
nous disons qui li
furent ainz qu'il
passassent la mer
el desert de etham empres de sur & empres de helim & empres de sim. Si alerent .iij. iourz par le desert et ne trou-
uerent nulle yaue. Dont vindrent il
en marach pour ce que elles estoient
ameres. De quoi moyses donna au lieu
propre non. Et lapela marach qui
vaut autant comme amertume. Dont
murmura li pueples encontre moyses. Et distrent que buuirons nous.
Et il cria a nostre seigneur. Et nostre
sires li moustra vne piece de fust que
nostre moyses mist en yaues. Et elles
furent muees en doucour. La donna
nostre sires aus ebrieus commandemens
et iugemenz. C'est a dire que il leur pro
mist a donner ce dist li maistres en istoi
res se il vousissent obeir a lui. Et leur
dist moyses se tu ois la vois de nostre
seigneur ton dieu. Et se tu fais droitu
re deuant lui. Et se tu obeis a ses comman
demens et tu les gardes. Je n'amenrai
mie de leur toi la languer que ie mis
en egypte. Car ie sui nostre sires li sau
ueres Des fontaines et des paumes
en helym selonc la bible. XXII

Donques vindrent il en helum la
ou il furent & la ou xij fontai
nes estoient. & lxx paumier. Si mistrent
leur heberges decoste les yaues. Ce
dist li maistres en hystoires que Jo
sephum dist que petit d'iaue estoit
es fontaines. Si comme l'iaue estoit
es fontaines. Et l'iaue que len en
ostoit estoit mout durement brai
euse et noient proufitable si que
li paumier estoient si tres durement
petis que il paroient mout tres pe
titement desseure terre. Car les hu
meurs des yaues des fontaines ne
souffisoient mie aus paumiers ar
rouser De la manne et des coutre
lieus selonc la bible. XXX

De helim s'en alerent
il tant que toute
la multitude des filz
israel s'en vindrent
tout droitement el
desert de sym qui est
entre helym et syna
y au quinziesme ior
du secont mois. Ce fu ce dist li mais
tres en istoires. Au trentiesme iour de
leur issue d'egypte. Ce est a dire com
ment il celebroient leur seconde pasque.
Si leur faillirent leur viandes. Et
toute l'assamblee des filz israel com
mencierent mout tres forment a mur
murer encontre moysem et aaron el
desert. & leur distrent. pleust a dieu q

4. Psalter, 1537: from the collections of Arundel, Harley, the Duchess of Portland, and Horace Walpole. (*See p.* 25)

The John Carter Brown Library, Brown University, Providence, R.I., MS. 7

9. Missal of Cardinal Domenico Della Rovere: miniature signed by Francesco de Castello. (*See p.* 58)

From the collections of Lord Thurlow, Edward Astle, W. Esdaile, J. B. Jarman, and Edouard Rahir. Pierpont Morgan Library, New York, MS. 306, f. 78[v]

10. William Roscoe, 1753–1831. (*See p.* 68)
Attributed to J. Williamson. National Portrait Gallery

11. The surrender of the Elector of Saxony to Charles V at the battle of Muhlberg in 1547, from Grenville's celebrated MS., The Victories of Charles V. (*See p.* 80)

British Museum, Add. MS. 33733, f. 15

12. Robert Curzon being tempted into extravagance by Payne and Foss. (*See p.* 91)
Pen drawing by Walter Sneyd, in Houghton Library, Harvard, bMS Eng. 1129

13. Sir Frederic Madden, 1833. (*See p.* 95)
Water-colour portrait by Richard Dighton. In the author's possession

14. Meeting of R. Curzon and Walter Sneyd after their return from foreign travel in search of antie manuscripts. (*See p.* 108)

Pen drawing by Walter Sneyd, in Houghton Library, Harvard, bMS Eng. 1129

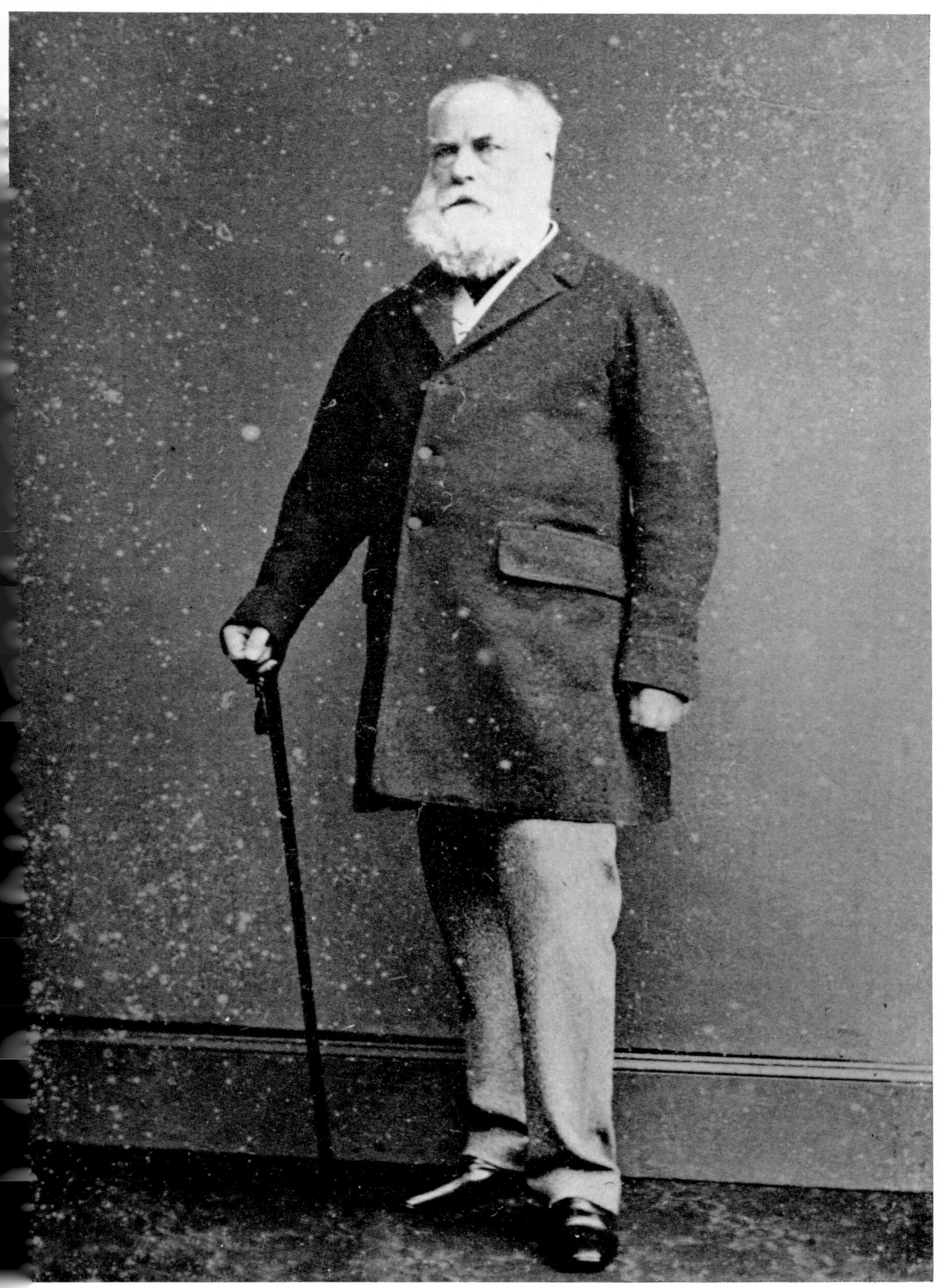

15. Bertram, 4th Earl of Ashburnham, 1797–1878. (*See p.* 121)
Enlargement from a carte-de-visite *photograph,* c. *1860, in the possession of the late J. R. Bickersteth*

16. Moses receiving the Law: miniature from the Alcuin Bible. (*See p.* 150)
British Museum, Add. MS. 10546, f. 25v

Her host led them through the long gallery at the top of the house, lined with pictures: he showed them the Priest's hole, and the Chapel, where they could not linger because of the icy cold. Then they walked round the ancient gardens with their yew hedges and across the park to one of the woods. As darkness fell in the great hall the suits of armour set up on lay figures seemed to come to life, and in the dusk it was easy for an imaginative child to detect eyes and manes in the headpieces of the iron-clad horses.

One of the things I liked best at Parham [she concluded] were the prayers that Lord Zouche read before we went to bed. He read them in the great hall: the servants stood in a long row at the other end, & from a very dim lamp & from the wood fire, so our end of the hall was all dim & ghost-like, for the fire flickered and the Knights came to life again, & moved their helmets. Then in the dead silence one heard Lord Zouche, rather far off reading prayers, and in the pause that followed each prayer the great clock ticked 'Forever-Never'. I looked the whole time at the stars; they were very bright, & Orion's belt hung in front of the window.

With regard to the family prayers, at that date of course a routine in most households, Curzon was, I believe, a man of deep religious conviction, who thought often and deeply about the fundamentals of his faith. I have found little to support this view in his letters, even to his closest friend, Sneyd, but I think he would have been one of the last men to indulge in those emotional passages of spiritual self-analysis which are such a feature of the correspondence of his period. Nevertheless, I bought some years ago in Windsor a manuscript of a curious nature which I found both interesting and moving. Curzon wrote this note at the beginning: 'The following pages contain the substance of a discussion which took place at Arundel and at Parham, between the Earl of Arundel, and Robert Curzon, in the year 1847. The greater part is in the handwriting of Lord Arundel, whose high minded character and noble honesty must be admired by those of every religion.'

The Lord Arundel in question became in 1856 the 19th Duke of Norfolk, and was well known for his support of Catholic charities, a man of great saintliness. The document I own would seem to represent an attempt by Lord Arundel to convert Curzon to Roman

Catholicism. He sets out on folio sheets various New Testament passages which support doctrinal points such as the Infallibility of the Church, Extreme Unction, Intercession of Saints, the Celibacy of the Clergy, and so on. Curzon, in his turn, has searched the New Testament for texts which, in his view, had a contrary tendency. Sheets containing the arguments for and against are bound up alternately, and sometimes one participant in this written debate will annotate the other's contribution. The rancour which so often accompanies theological controversy is entirely lacking. Curzon obviously valued this exchange of views highly: he had it bound in full red morocco, lettered 'Articles of Faith', with his arms on the covers, and inserted in it many of the obituary notices of the Duke which appeared at his death in 1860. One cannot handle it without gaining the impression that here were two devout and honourable men, anxiously seeking for the Truth.

In February 1873 Curzon wrote to tell Sneyd that he had received a very bad report from his doctor, and that he might not survive long. Letters which followed show a sharp and progressive deterioration of his handwriting, and on 2 August the most attractive figure in the annals of book-collecting took leave of his beloved Parham. The fourteenth volume of *Philobiblon Society Miscellanies* contains a moving obituary of him, anonymous, but almost certainly one in which Sneyd must have had a major share. The obituarist dwells on Curzon's gaiety, originality, and frankness.

All concealment of thought was foreign to his nature, and while in consequence of an imperfect education, he would sometimes make blunders as to matters of rather ordinary classical & modern political knowledge, his naturally quick understanding, his love of perspicuity, his simplicity and scorn of ornament, his determination to state the impression he had formed, whatever prejudice it might affront, often rendered his conversation not only very interesting and original, but occasionally very instructive . . . The foundation of his character was sincerity, which but for his natural good breeding and desire to avoid inflicting pain might sometimes have given offence; but so checked and tempered it laid the foundation of those few but steady and loving friendships which cheered his often very chequered life.

The Philobiblon Society was another interest in which the friends had both shared. Founded in 1853, this flourishing group of book-collectors owed much of its success to Richard Monckton Milnes, in the second volume of whose life by Mr. James Pope-Hennessy will be found the best short account available of the Society's activities.[1] For the Duc d'Aumale,[2] the Society's patron, Curzon had a warm regard. 'Besides being a Prince he is the most intelligent man of the club, & knows more about books, & pictures, & what is what, than most of us', he wrote to Sneyd in 1857. Both he and Sneyd were members and both contributed papers to the *Miscellanies*.[3]

Of Curzon's contributions, perhaps the most interesting is his 'History of Printing in China and Europe'. He explains that when the Earl of Elgin set out on a mission to China in 1857 he had asked him to make inquiries about various ancient Chinese inventions, the mariner's compass, gunpowder, fireworks, distilling, and printing. Elgin secured some information about the last from Thomas Taylor Meadows in a long letter dated from Ningpo on 5 April 1858, which Curzon describes as the first authentic account to be brought to Europe of the rise and progress of the art in China. Meadows gave Elgin a copy of a book printed in 1415, and cited evidence from various Chinese historical works to show that printing was invented in China about A.D. 860. Curzon then goes on to trace its origins in Europe, through inscriptions stamped on Roman pottery and lead, thence to various *codices purpurei*, which he mistakenly thought were stamped or stencilled and not written, thence to block-books and stamped outlines of initials on Papal documents, and so to Gutenberg, Donatus fragments, and movable type. Curzon also describes the fragments of what were thought to be parts of Gutenberg's press,

[1] *The Flight of Youth*, 1951, pp. 39–43.

[2] The fifth son of Louis-Philippe, part of whose splendid library was at Twickenham when the Duke was living in what Lord Houghton called 'sumptuous and studious exile' in this country. I possess an unpublished manuscript by John Holmes of the British Museum, 'A short Notice of some MSS. belonging to the Duc d'Aumale', which the author gave to Lord Ashburnham in May 1849. The manuscripts, now at Chantilly, were valued by the Duke in 1849 at £18,000.

[3] Curzon's contributions were: in vol. 1, 'A short Account of some of the most celebrated Libraries of Italy'; vol. 2, 'The Book of the Prophet Moses and the History of the Prophet Moses'; vol. 6, 'History of Printing in China and Europe'; vol. 9, 'The Lord Mayor's Visit to Oxford, July 1826, etc.'.

dated 1441, which had been discovered at Mainz in March 1856 and which he had sketched on the spot in July of the same year.

The same interesting, if slightly uncritical, mingling of first-hand observation and questionable secondary sources is to be found in Curzon's other valuable contribution to the *Miscellanies*, 'A short Account of some of the most celebrated Libraries of Italy', in which he gives notes on the manuscripts in nearly a dozen libraries, made from personal inspection mostly during the eighteen-forties. I bought some time ago one of twenty-five offprints of this work which he had sent to his cousin, T. L. Parker, with a highly characteristic letter, dated 21 March 1855:

> Here is the history of the New Philobiblon Society. Those members who can write have a little dab of literature printed, and these various contributions together form a goodly volume which those members who *can read* may peruse at their leisure. The Philobiblon volume is to come out once a year; the Duc d'Aumale sent a very interesting paper, several pages longer than mine which I enclose for your edification. The *breakfasts* have been remarkably interesting & agreeable, that at the Duc d'Aumale's naturally the most so, as he inherited all the treasures of the great house of Condé. We have no dinners, and so long as we do not admit any members who don't care about old books, it will be a flourishing little society. It has answered wonderfully well hitherto.
>
> The Roxburghe Club of which I have the sad misfortune to be a member, is a dreadful failure for this reason, they have the folly to elect no end of great magnificos, who neither know or care anything about the matter, so there is no esprit de corps, and you have a most stupid dinner for which I paid last time £4. 19. 6 for my one plate, & I could not have got through a pound's worth, if I had been as drunk as an owl.[1]

The middle of the nineteenth century was certainly rather a torpid period in the Roxburghe Club's history. Curzon's keen sense of the ridiculous undoubtedly dictated his choice of the book he himself presented to the Club, an edition by Dr. Furnivall of three early gastronomical tracts, with a tilt at the Club itself in the irrepressible

[1] Curzon's wit and high spirits can also be found in the early poetical pastiche he wrote in collaboration with Reginald Heber, *The Lay of the Purple Falcon* (B.M. Add. MS. 39669; printed by William Nicol in 1847), in which he catches to perfection the naïveté, the inconsequentiality, and especially the crashing anti-climaxes of bad fifteenth-century verse.

editor's preface. 'I send you the Boke of Nurture, as also ye Boke of Kervynge', Curzon wrote to Sneyd on 28 September 1867, 'of which right worthi and profitable bokes 40 copies have been printed, besides one on vellum.[1] . . . I hope it is not quite so stupid and unreadable as many of the Roxburghe books. As the members of that effete society never meet except once a year, at a very expensive dinner, I thought the subject of the book was appropriate.'

I turn now to the friends' collections, to Curzon's first, and will confine myself mainly to his manuscripts. Both men were already collecting as undergraduates at Oxford. Three of Curzon's Western manuscripts contain on the flyleaf his name and college and the accession date 1829. In October 1830 he was book-hunting in Leipzig, and I own a bibliographical reference book which J. A. G. Weigel, a bookseller of that town, gave him during this visit, on the blank leaves of which the recipient has made notes on remarkable manuscripts and block-books in Weigel's stock.[2] In the following year he was combing Paris, and one of the earliest letters to Sneyd is written just after his return to England: the mood is rhapsodical—'oh la bibliothèque, oh De Bure!' Curzon's letters have to be read with caution, for he was an inveterate leg-puller, and it was his whimsical pleasure on at least one occasion to write and thank Sneyd for a number of very expensive but imaginary gifts from Payne and Foss's latest catalogue (Plate 12). On 29 March 1832 he sent Sneyd a genuine list of seven important purchases, among them an early manuscript of Lydgate's 'Falls of Princes' (a translation of Boccaccio's 'De Casibus Virorum Illustrium'), a Hebrew roll containing the Book of Esther, the first printed German Bible, and four books printed on vellum, including an illuminated copy of Fust and Schoeffer's *Constitutiones* of Clement, 1471. A month later he reported that De Bure was sending him a Jarry manuscript on approval for '3 times its weight in gold', doubtless the *Office de la Vierge*, 1659, with miniatures, of which he became the proud owner.[3] In July of the same year preparations were afoot for

[1] Major J. R. Abbey owned this copy and gave it to the Library of the Roxburghe Club.
[2] W. Hebenstreit, *Dictionarium Editionum Auctorum Classicorum*, 8°, Vindobonae, 1828.
[3] B.M. Add. MS. 39642.

a joint holiday in Germany, during which a number of purchases were made.

Some of Curzon's most fascinating letters to his friend were written in the course of his journeys in the Middle East. They are important as showing the raw materials which were worked up with such artistry into Curzon's great travel book, but quotation from them here must obviously be limited, the more so since it is greatly to be hoped that Mr. Ian Fraser will in due course publish them in full. Here, for example, is his account of the visit to the monastery of St. Catherine on Sinai, made during his first tour in 1833–4, and extracted from a long letter written from Cairo in March 1834.

If I ever ride a camel or a dromedary again may I be —. I have torn all my clothes, spoiled my gun, rubbed several holes in my posteriors, and the sun has taken all the skin off my face, during my pilgrimage to Gebel el Tour, or as it is called by the good people in Europe Mount Sinai. Like the children of Israel I passed from Cairo *through* the Red Sea and jogged across the wilderness of Sin Tor many days, seeing nothing but sand and rock and the savage Bedouins who accompanied by camels. At last I got to the end of my journey and was pulled up through a window at the end of a long rope and found myself surrounded by the good Fathers in the Monastery of St Catherine. Now you must know that 'I had heard of books, and I longed to rescue from the shelf some sturdy tome,'[1] so after remaining some little time in the Monastery I began to rummage about to see what I could devour, and at length found the library with a curious old door inlaid with iron, and about 1500 mss., original old books, arranged on shelves around the wall. The first book I saw was the Gospels, a ms. in Greek on vellum of the 10th century with a great iron cross hammered onto the binding with 6 good large nails: another tome was a Greek ms. of the Psalms with Byzantine illuminations representing King David & others scratching some horrible old harps as if their only hopes of salvation depend on the music they produced. 1000 other Greek mss. contributed to excite my cupidity and cover me with dust, and I was nearly overwhelmed by a prodigious volume of the 'lives of the Saints' which fell like an avalanche from the upper shelf carrying whole legions of duodecimos in its train which fluttered about in the dust and settled peaceably at last upon the floor. After this I saw in another room a book

[1] A quotation from Dibdin, whom the two friends regarded as a considerable figure of fun.

which, Oh Sneyd, look upon me as a sainted man, a kind of paragon of virtue among Bibliomaniacs when I tell you that I did not steal—a thick old 4to manuscript of the Gospels, written in gold uncial letters in Greek, in a silver gilt binding, and illuminated by the antient Romans of that ilk, when the book was presented to the library by (I think Honorius) the Emperor of Rome, a certain King as the superior had heard who lived sometime ago at Constantinople. Afterwards I got the old superior into his own room and offered him no end of piastres for some of the books, but *ΑΡΙΣΤΕ* said the superior you should have any of them, only unluckily a certain Englishman[1] took several of them away about 15 years ago, and only gave the Monastery a telescope in exchange, in consequence of which the late superior was degraded to the level of a common monk, and that is a trifle to what they will do to me if I sell you any of them, at any price. But I will give you half a dozen of liqueur, said I. Liqueur, said he, ah where is it? So I gave it him on the spot. This is excellent, said the superior. Yes, and nobody will know anything about it, said I. But there is a catalogue and you can't have any books at all, and so the old rogue drank the good Rosolio and I did not get a book after all though I went to Mount Sinai on purpose to get them. In fact there is no chance of getting anything out of a Greek so I trotted sulkily home again to Cairo, with a little box of Manna & 2 tables of stone on which Moses is to write the Commandments for me when I get back to England. This is one of the many disappointments I have experienced here where nothing that I have undertaken ever seems to succeed. I have got no antiquities of any consequence, and am sore all over with a sort of boil which attacks people in Egypt and prevents my sleeping, sitting down [or] doing anything else, so I hope some of my sins will be [forgiven] me in consideration thereof. For everybody has brought trea[sure out of] Egypt except me.[2]

Curzon did, however, contrive to make some purchases during his first visit to the Middle East: in particular he acquired a group of

[1] I am most grateful to Mr. T. C. Skeat and Dr. C. E. Wright for their tentative identification of this traveller as William John Bankes, who visited St. Catherine's monastery in 1815, and 'by persevering and rummaging found out a library of 2,000 volumes'. See W. Turner, *Journal of a Tour in Levant*, ii, 1820, pp. 443–4 n. Bankes brought away five MSS., including an *Iliad*, part of Aeschylus, the *Medea* of Euripides, and the *Physics* of Aristotle. See V. N. Bénéchevitch, *Les Mss. grecs du Mont Sinai et le monde savant de l'Europe depuis le XVIIe siècle jusqu'à 1927*, Texte und Forschungen zur Byzantinisch-Neugriechischen Philologie, no. 21, Athens, 1937, p. 15.

[2] Fraser No. 24.

manuscripts from the monastery at St. Sabba, near Jerusalem, and others on Mount Athos. Early in 1835 he unpacked his accessions in London.

I have opened my box [he wrote to Sneyd], even the big box of old Mss., Papyri and other sweetmeats; then I went to Mr Payne & Foss and there was received with exceeding great glory by Foss and with a kind of bland condescension on the part of Payne; then I axed him to come and see me, which he did accordingly, and groaned and turned up the white of his eyes at the sight of such *θησαυροι*. He offered me a splendid copy of the *Biblia Pauperum* for the most seedy MS. but I wanted to have the famous *Monte Santo de Dio* into the bargain;[1] so this important bargain is not yet concluded, & I walk about the street with the air of a man who is somebody and has a thing or two, 'spicially a tome'. . . . Yours very sincerely

Wynkyn de Worde[2]

Another visitor with even higher standards was equally impressed. On 8 May 1836 Sir Frederic Madden called at 26 Upper Brook Street. He particularly admired the Greek manuscripts and noted down the presence of

two copies of the Gospels, one very beautiful written A.C. 1009, a copy of the first 8 books of the Old Test[ament] of the 10 cent., a copy of the Acts and Epistles, an Evangelistarium, saec. 12, and several others of the 13 and 14 centuries. The Latin MSS. were of inferior interest, and were chiefly purchased in England. Mr C[urzon] showed me also a fine MS. of Lydgate's Boccace, several well preserved Egyptian papyri, some Babylonian cylinders, a beautiful copy of Caxton's Lyfe of St. Catherine, &c. He is quite a young man, and, from the zeal and judgement he has shown in making this collection, promises fair to be the *Harley* of some future period.[3]

Curzon took an equally favourable view of Madden's acumen, though he expressed it rather differently.

[1] Antonio [Bettini] da Siena: *Monte santo di Dio*, Florence, 1477, containing the first known book illustrations engraved on copper.

[2] Fraser No. 55. There is an ambiguity about the date of this letter, 21 Feb. 183[?]. The last digit appears to be 4 or 7. Mr. Fraser opts for the last, but from internal evidence 1835 seems more likely, and Mr. Fraser concurs in this emendation.

[3] Madden's journal for 8 May 1836: Bodleian MS. Eng. hist. c. 151, pp. 136–7.

'Sir Frederic Madden', he wrote to Sneyd on 13 May, 'is a young man with large whiskers & a smart stick & a waistcoat, & does not look half as much of a Bibliomaniac as you do, but notwithstanding his appearance is uncommon sly and knows more about the matter than anyone whom I have seen, except Angelo Mai[1] perhaps.'[2]

I had often tried to reconcile this picture of Madden, the dandy, with the portrait of the Keeper which hangs in the Students Room in the Department of Manuscripts at the British Museum, from which Madden peers studiously through his narrow-rimmed glasses. Certainly the whiskers and coiffure are rather elaborate, but one does not get the impression of a highly fashionable figure. And then I had a present which made all plain, when my friends Lionel and Philip Robinson gave me a water-colour portrait of Madden painted by Dighton in 1833 (Plate 13); here were all the points Curzon observed —the glossy whiskers, stick, eye-glass, signet-ring, cravat—as well as an endorsement in the hand of Sir Thomas Phillipps testifying that the likeness was a very faithful one.

In 1837, when Sir Thomas Phillipps printed a brief account of Curzon's manuscripts in his *Catalogus Manuscriptorum Magnae Britanniae*, forty-seven items were listed, thirteen Oriental manuscripts including eight papyri, seventeen Greek, and the rest Latin. Of the two friends, Sneyd was the first to set eyes on the already fabulous Sir Thomas at the Heber sale in February 1836, and, when he hastened to report this to Curzon, he received an enthusiastic reply, written from Hagley on 24 February.

Why did you not rush at him and shake him by the hand [asked Curzon], and with tears in your eyes tell him how glad you was of the opportunity of rendering hommage [*sic*] to the great autocrat of forgotten literature? I should like to have seen him enter the room. How Mr Evans must have bobbed his head, how Payne and Foss must have made their best joint bow in partnership & old Thorpe swung himself twice round at least, I have no doubt, when he made way to the greatest collector of the day. By the soul of Caxton, what a fine sight it must have been to see him walk out of the auction room when the sale was over with all the greatest men of the place bearing illuminated romances, and grim folios of the

[1] Cardinal Angelo Mai, 1782–1854, Librarian of the Vatican.

[2] Fraser No. 46.

10th century to his carriage at the door . . . surely it is a glorious thing to be the first man of ones line.[1]

Both young men made the great collector's acquaintance soon afterwards, and in Curzon's case a lifelong friendship developed. I do not think that any other man attracted Phillipps to the same degree, and his letters to Curzon have a warmth and geniality, and a lack of his congenital irascibility, which make them almost unique. I have devoted Chapter VI in the third volume of my *Phillipps Studies* to this subject and do not wish to repeat myself here: but when Curzon set off on his greatest and most successful book-hunting expedition in May 1837, the Baronet had formed the design of marrying his eldest daughter to the young man whose interests so nearly coincided with his own, a situation from which Curzon extricated himself with the greatest tact and delicacy.

Curzon's letters written to Sneyd during his second tour of the Levant are rather fragmentary, but quotation from two or three of them is irresistible. In one he describes his purchases at Thebes, adding that Dibdin would have written a 'Theban Nosegay' on the subject immediately. 'You know I want to have', he wrote, '100 manuscript *books*, as specimens of writing at different times, and I think I now have 60, which are good ones, and average £25 apiece in value, besides the rest of the seedy tomes which I bought formerly, & which I do not count in the collection.'[2]

In another letter he gives an ecstatic account of the treasures in the library of St. John at Patmos. After describing in some detail ten of the finest manuscripts, he continues:

The library contains many other splendid books but the 10 which I have mentioned surpass everything at Mt. Athos or anywhere else except perhaps the Bulgarian MS. which I have sent home, for in its way that is not to be surpassed.[3] Of course I offered all my money & my other coat & my old hat and my little finger for these literary wonders but alas all to no purpose. So I wrote to Lord Ponsonby in despair & begged him to declare war with the Sultan immediately, if the books were not sold to me, & to hang all the monks he could find till that desirable end was accomplished . . . I wish Queen Victoria could send for them; it is really

[1] Fraser No. 44. [2] Fraser No. 62. [3] B.M. Add. MS. 39627.

a shame to leave them where they are, rotting in a monastic library where no one cares about them. If I do not get them they will fall into the hands of the first Russian who cares to have them, for they do not stick at a trifle when they find anything worth having in these regions. With a dejected countenance I walked down the hill from the Great Monastery to the chapel over the cave where St John wrote the Apocalypse. They showed me there a leaf of papyrus in the Hieratic Character which they said was part of the original ms. of the Revelations in St John's handwriting. This for years has been adored by pilgrims as a relic of the Evangelist, but on my explaining to the multitude that it could never have been written by St John, seeing that it was 1000 years older than his days, they let me take it away & I shall preserve it as a memorial of the extraordinary things I saw in the library of St John at Patmos.[1]

Few passages in Curzon's letters, however, can surpass in interest his account, written on the Nile 'between Ionani & Otfe' and completed in Alexandria on 3 April 1838, of his visit to the monastery of Souriani on the Natron Lakes, which provides one of the most dramatic episodes in Curzon's book. There are significant differences between this account, written just after the event, and the polished narrative of a dozen years later.[2] In particular the well-known passage where Curzon plies the old blind abbot with rosolio does not feature in this first version. He begins by saying that a further purchase of books demands a new letter to his 'fellow bibliologist', especially an accession of Syriac and Coptic manuscripts, some of which he describes, particularly extolling a fragment of the Gospels in Coptic. 'The place I discovered it, and the manner of the lugging it away on the back of a camel across the desert merits a particular description', he adds, and he sets the stage by recounting his trip across the Libyan desert to the ancient monastery of Souriani, a 'doleful place', according to Curzon, with a huge square tower. Having visited the dark chapel, with its pictures of saints 'of sad aspect', he crossed the vaulted passage to the library, where he found the copy of the Coptic Gospels.

Here I saw no Syriac books [he continued], and after asking if they had none, some said they had, some said they had not, till at last, an old blind

[1] Fraser No. 61. [2] *Visits to Monasteries in the Levant*, Chapters VII and VIII.

monk sent for candles, and led the way down a dark winding staircase to the lower story of the tower; we stumbled over various great jars, where the early fathers used to keep their oil, and squeezing through a low narrow door, I found myself with 2 monks, holding candles, in an arched dungeon, full of books. They were strewn upon the floor, most of them all torn, and loose from the trammels of their bindings, piled upon each other in inextricable confusion. Down I went upon my knees, and, taking off my upper garments, plunged into the mass of dust and parchment, now seizing a fat quarto by the middle, which fell to pieces in my hands, and then pulling out a number of leaves, nearly a yard long, belonging to some magnificent, but ruined, manuscript. In course of time I caught a perfect tome, and then another and one of the monks pulled out a third from under an immense heap of fragments. I could find no more, and while pausing to rest from the labours of my search, with a candle in each hand I saw the two monks tugging away at something with all their might. 'fi waked somedook', here is a box, said one. Is there? cried the Superior from without, for the first time feeling any interest in our occupation. A box, shouted the rest, what is there in it, do not open it in there, bring it out; we will all see what it contains. It is cruel heavy, sighed the 2 monks within; till having cleared it from the piles of literature which weighed it down, they dragged out no box, but the thundering old volume I have told you of above. The poor monks were sadly disappointed. Give it to the Frank, said the Superior, what can he see in these cursed books? Here come away, there is no use rummaging there any more; there is nothing worth having there, come out. Out we came all laden with dust and manuscripts. A monk not feeling quite certain about the great book, when it was produced, opened it, and, seeing it really was no box, shut it with a bang, and climbed up the steep staircase after his brethren. I had these Syriac folios taken to my room, and after a long conversation got them all, and the 3 Coptic ones into the bargain for 400 piastres, about 4.4.0, and, ordering my camels to be loaded early the next morning, set out upon my way rejoicing.[1]

A list of the manuscripts collected by Curzon in Egypt in 1838 is attached to this letter, seventeen Arabic, two Persian, fifteen Coptic, four Syriac, and two Abyssinian.

Curzon spent the winter of 1839–40 at Naples with Lord De Tabley, his friend from Christ Church days. The following year he

[1] Fraser No. 63.

took up the diplomatic post to which I referred above, and gathered, mostly in 1843, the materials for his second travel book, *Armenia*. On this expedition also he wrote a number of letters to Sneyd which are at Keele. During 1846 he spent some time in Italy examining manuscripts, especially in the Vatican. Two letters to Sneyd of 1847 give some account of the origin and progress of the book on which his fame chiefly rests.

I have employed myself [he wrote from Parham on Easter Sunday] with writing an opusculum which has swelled to vast bulk, considering my dislike to quill driving. When I go to Town I shall try to get somebody to read it and see whether it is worth printing: It contains:— 1. a lyttell tretyse on writing. 2. history of curious out of the way libraries. 3. catalogue of my own oriental books and old stones, &c. 4. adventures and history of Mount Athos. 5. Ditto Holy Land, and there should be 6 and 7, of Albania and the Coptic Monasteries in Egypt and Africa. There are about 300 quarto printed pages written. I wish I knew who could look it over for me,—and who would give me 100,000£ for it afterwards.[1]

It will be observed that at this stage Curzon envisaged as a single work what in fact became two, the *Visits to Monasteries in the Levant* and his privately printed *Catalogue of Materials for Writing*. A few weeks later, however, the plan of making a separate volume of sections 4–7 seems to have been evolved.

I wrote no end of Ms., I think I told you, during Lent at Parham [he reported to Sneyd from 50 Berkeley Square on 8 May], and I took it the other day to Mr Murray and he says he will publish it at Xmas, 1000 copies, and give me half the profits; only he makes an ugly condition, which spoils it all, and that is that I must write 200 pages more, what he has got now being only 350; now the very notion of writing 200 pages is enough to frighten one out of one's wits . . .[2]

The immediate and enduring success of Curzon's book needs no stressing here. It has brought delight to generations of book collectors as well as to devotees of the literature of travel. The most romantic copy extant is still at Parham; it is the one which Curzon gave to

[1] Fraser No. 152: 4 Apr. 1847.

[2] Fraser No. 155.

Emily Wilmot-Horton, and it contains an inscription in which the author offers his book—and himself—to his future bride.

Curzon's *Catalogue of Materials for Writing* also appeared in 1849, a slim folio, excellently printed for the author at William Nicol's Shakespeare Press, with twelve plates. It is a rare book, fifty copies only having been printed. In his Preface Curzon explains that the collection has been put at the disposal of Biblical and other scholars, and that his prime purpose was to illustrate the origin and progress of the arts of writing and illumination 'of distant nations and of antient days'. If the reader bears this motive in mind, he adds, 'it is hoped that the possessor of these Manuscripts may escape in some measure the imputation of folly, which is given to those Bibliomaniacs, who heap up accumulations of old books which they can neither use nor understand'. Curzon, of course, had a working knowledge of a number of languages, but he made no claim to profound scholarship. He had, however, a true feeling of veneration for antiquity, an agile and inquiring mind, and a flair for recognizing at sight important manuscripts among hundreds of lesser interest; and that sixth sense, which enables a collector correctly to evaluate an ancient manuscript on its general appearance rather than after detailed study of its contents, is the subject of a well-known passage in the seventeenth chapter of his *Armenia*.[1] Far the most interesting copy of Curzon's *Catalogue* is his own interleaved and profusely annotated example, which is in the Department of Manuscripts, the British Museum.[2] From it one learns that it cost £150 to produce, but that £100 of this figure was the expense of the lithographic facsimiles, and one discovers how the greater part of the edition was distributed. Among the recipients of presentation copies were Lords Ashburnham and Vernon, Sneyd, Phillipps, Beriah Botfield, Evelyn Philip Shirley, and the Pope. Thorpe was given twenty-three copies to sell, and there is an inserted letter from his son naming the purchasers of eight of these, and adding that, since his late father's estate was only paying four shillings in the pound, Curzon's share of the money owing to him amounted to £6. 3*s.* 0*d.* Numerous manuscript additions bring the total number of items in the *Catalogue* to 284,

[1] *Armenia*, 1854 edn., pp. 237–40.

[2] K.R. 10. d.

and these Curzon values at £5,000, allowing £1,000 for the Bulgarian Gospels (No. 153). In addition to the printed Preface there is a manuscript foreword in which he sets down clearly his purpose in forming such a library:

In making the following collection, it is my object to illustrate the rise and progress of the art of writing, from the time when laws or histories were inscribed on any portable substances to the present day—tracing the improvements and alteration of different ages and nations, both in the materials on which they wrote and the manner in which the original drawings and hieroglyphics gradually assumed the form of perfect Alphabets. From thence I proceed to the earlier Manuscripts in the form of Tablets, Rolls and Books, showing the various styles of writing and illumination through the dark ages, till we arrive at the perfection of the art displayed in the gorgeous folios of the 15th century . . .

By a natural process Curzon then continued the series by including specimens of printing and engraving. In order to keep it in as small a compass as he could, he reduced it to three divisions, each planned to contain not more than about 200 specimens. The first embraced hieroglyphics, clay tablets, engraved gems, and manuscripts on various substances in the form of rolls; the second manuscript books proper; and the third early printing.

'The whole will form', he adds, 'a kind of preface to a modern library, and will enable anyone who may be curious in such matters to survey with one glance the various channels through which the mighty stream of literature has flowed on.' He concludes on a note of pessimism. 'Writing', he asserts, 'is the cause of many disasters—and so much sorrow and discontent, that it is almost to be wished that so treacherous an art had never been invented. Like all great men, and great discoveries, it is more famous for the injuries it has done to mankind than for the good it has bestowed on the human race . . .', and he ends by disparaging the much vaunted 'March of Intellect'.

From his printed catalogue Curzon specifically excludes all Western manuscripts except Greek. His first section is of writing materials, including a *cuir-bouilli* pen-case traditionally owned by Henry VI; then follow early writings on wood, stone, clay, and pottery. The next division is of his rolled manuscripts, on papyrus, linen, and vellum, with a few other Oriental manuscripts not in the *codex* form. Then begin the *codices* proper, Hebrew, Syriac (including three of great antiquity), Arabic, Tartar, Turkish, Persian, Armenian (among them a magnificent thirteenth-century Bible), Hindustani, Abyssinian, Greek (among them several written before A.D. 1000, and a wonderful Gospel Lectionary said to have been written by the Emperor Alexius Comnenus),[1] Coptic (including three more truly venerable volumes), and finally Bulgarian, a class which contained the superbly decorated copy of the Gospels,[2] given him at the Monastery of SS. Paul and George on Mount Athos, 'probably one of the most interesting MSS.', he notes with pardonable pride, 'that has been brought to England for many years'. Manuscript additions in his own copy extend the range of languages to Chinese, Georgian, and Aztec, and he has added lists of his Latin manuscripts, twenty-two in number, and those in modern languages, eighteen. The latter class contains, besides such things as his favourite Jarry manuscript, one or two unexpected items, the autograph manuscript of Walter Scott's earliest ballad, for example; and the collector's own autograph journals of his tours in Egypt, Syria, Greece, and Arabia, still in the possession of his descendants. There is also a list of what he regarded as the most interesting of his printed books, three Caxtons, nine Wynkyn de Wordes, a group of English romances, such as *Valentine and Orson* and *Palmerin of England*, a series of chronicles, the four Shakespeare folios, and some important incunabula, among them the Subiaco Lactantius of 1465, the Valturius of 1471, *Monte Santo di Dio*, 1477, the first book illustrated with copper engravings, the 1481 Dante, the 1486 Breydenbach, and the *editio princeps* of Homer. From these manuscript lists there are some important books omitted which he certainly owned, among them a very fine set of De Bry's Voyages. This perhaps is the point to confess that I have no note of exactly when he acquired his copy of the 42-line Bible. It was a defective mutilated example from Mannheim which the Royal Library at Munich sold as a duplicate on 23 August 1832, but whether directly to Curzon I have not ascertained. After the Zouche

[1] B.M. Add. MS. 39603.

[2] B.M. Add. MS. 39627.

sale at Sotheby's in November 1920 it was bought by Gabriel Wells, dismembered, and converted into a number of 'Noble Fragments' with a prefatory encomium by A. Edward Newton.

The tempo of Curzon's collecting did not slacken with advancing years. On 7 November 1859 he reported to Sneyd one of his most valuable accessions, 'a very fine Aztec manuscript; it is about 30 feet long, and covered on both sides with frightful figures of horrible Americans, beautifully done, tho' in a strange style, in bright colours. I have been after this tome for many years . . . the most curious, and certainly the most entirely incomprehensible wollum that I have got.' This was the famous Zouche codex, reproduced in facsimile by the Peabody Museum in 1902.[1] It had been in the library of the Dominican monastery of San Marco in Florence, and Curzon had been angling for it for some years, finally securing it in 1859.

Two years later he acquired a papyrus in a distinctly unusual way. 'I think the following extracts from the Chronicon Gimcrackense may be interesting to you. So here goes', he wrote to his friend on 25 November 1861.

On Friday last Mr Foss took me to Signor Libri's house, near the British Museum, a nice airy house, and not a blessed book to be seen. However first Mr Foss had a glass of wine, & then another, & at last we became interested on the subject of tomes, & Mr Libri took us up to his den at the top of the house, and 'there are tomes,' 8 books in jewelled & enamelled binding, others in Grolier, & wonderful coverings, beautifully illuminated MSS., &c., &c., &c., such as one seldom sees. I cannot imagine where he can have got such splendid things in these ransacked days. I was surprised to find (tho' I said nothing) that so learned, and evidently very clever a man had been cheated, in 2 or 3 instances; the ivories in what he called his best book cover, a large folio, were sham, & so were a whole drawer full of Coptic papyri. We became great friends, for he appreciated my zeal and admiration of his books, &, as we were going away, he gave me, in a way I did not know how to refuse, the only genuine papyrus that I saw there; it is about 7 feet long, in hieroglyphics, partly in coarse bright colours. As I have above 20 papyri already I was sorry to take it, but I thought he might be offended if I refused. So I hope to unroll it when I get to Parham, and it is an interesting memorial of the donor.[2]

[1] B.M. Add. MS. 39671.

[3] Fraser No. 320.

Within five years of his death an important manuscript was acquired by chance after a visit to Walmer in Kent, and the collector hastened to describe his coup to Sneyd in his best epistolary vein.

On my way back through Dover on Monday [he wrote on 15 October 1868] I bought a wonderful Abyssinian Ms., a great big 4$^{to.}$ on vellum, with 40 large hideous pictures of the miracles of our Saviour. It is in fact King Theodore's Bible,[1] and was plundered from his palace or hut at Magdala by a soldier, who sold it to an extortioner, from whom I got it, for a tenpunnote. As I was sweltering down the street with this lumbering old tome under my arm, (it was a hot close day) I thought how my dear old Abbot would laugh, if he saw me pounding along with a cloak and an umbrella on my way to the station, resting my precious bundle on the sill of a window every now & then, for it weighs about a ton & stinks like pison. For I refused the proffered services of a small boy to carry the big book, and I was glad at last when I landed it safely in the train which took Lord Ebury, the Dean of Westminster & the Emperor Theodore's voluminous volume back to Folkestone. Nothing can exceed the grimness of the flaring illuminations of the Abyssinian artist; each of them had a very dirty rag to cover it, and, when I had sent them all to the Kitchen fire, it did not smell quite so much as before, and I think, when it has been brushed up by the binder, it will be quite pleasant . . .[2]

No book collector can be indifferent to the infectious gaiety and enthusiasm of Curzon's letters. In 1852 he wrote ecstatically of his purchases from a catalogue of Cornish Brothers of Birmingham, who had under-priced their wares because, according to Curzon, they had not discovered 'that Wynandus de Worde was the same gent as Wynkyn de Worde'. The volume in question was a Terence —I suppose the *Vulgaria Terentii* of 1529: at all events it was a bargain at 10*s.* 0*d.* even in 1852. In 1869 the collector reported 'a new fit of Bibliomania', which led him to buy a copy of the Coverdale Bible, and then to negotiate for other Bibles with Francis Fry, 'a Quaker, and a maker of Chocolate and Bibles, which he makes up from imperfect copies'. Not the least entertaining features of Curzon's style are these shrewd, witty, and often irreverent appraisals of familiar characters. Ruskin, for example, in 1854, was 'a clever

[1] B.M. Or. MS. 8824.

[2] Fraser No. 409.

odd sort of fellow, but I believe he never was at school to have the natural self-sufficiency kicked out of him, so he lays down the law with a loud voice, on subjects which his hearers may understand better than him. *Mrs* Ruskin is a duck, very pretty, very smart both in word & dress.'[1]

Whenever one of the friends visited the library of a fellow collector it was his practice to send the other an account of what he had seen. Sneyd's report to Curzon of his visit to the Duke of Hamilton in 1854 has unfortunately not come my way, but it evoked an enthusiastic reply, which begins: 'Well it is a fine thing to be a Duke with no end of £. S. D., tenements, messuages and genuine articles as Mr G. Robins[2] used to put it.' Also missing from the files is Curzon's account of his visit to Lord Ashburnham in 1847, a document Sneyd was urged to return to the writer, a request with which, unhappily for posterity, he complied, for it is not among the papers at Keele. Curzon's description, however, of his visit to Algernon Perkins, of Hanworth Park, near Richmond, survives in a letter of 9 May 1865. Perkins, Curzon explained, was the head of Barclay and Perkins's brewery, with a reputed income of £30,000 a year. 'His father collected books', he continued, 'and they really are wonderful to behold. He has not so many rare books, 2 or 300, if so many, but they are something like tomes, viz. the Mazarine Bible on vellum, in the original binding, with Gothic clasps, corners & bosses.' He goes on to describe the other superlative treasures which are familiar to us from the Perkins sale catalogue of June 1873. 'Mr Perkins does not take any interest in these magnificent books', he concluded, 'but will not sell them, tho' he says they probably will be sold at his death. This collection was bought mostly from old Thorpe, and is exactly what you and I should have got, if we had had beer enough, 35 years ago.'[3]

Robert Curzon's collection of manuscripts is not perhaps central to the subject of this book, but he was unique in his day as a connoisseur who assembled systematically a choice group of materials

[1] Fraser No. 231.

[2] The auctioneer of the contents of Strawberry Hill in 1842, famous for his promotional hyperbole.

[3] Fraser No. 360.

to illustrate the history of the arts of the writing and decoration of the book in all countries and periods. This was a highly original conception; and Curzon is worthy of more study as a collector than he has hitherto received. The availability of his own master-copy of his catalogue alongside his manuscripts[1] themselves, together with this long series of his enchanting letters at Keele, would make an extended treatment of him richly rewarding.

'Let Curzon holde what Curzon helde.' The proud family motto, employed by Curzon in his armorial book-stamp, seems singularly unapt when one sees it on some volume alienated from the Curzon library, and divorced from its shelf in his beloved Parham, which itself has passed into other hands. Certain things, however, which Robert Curzon held in his lifetime he holds to this day—a circle of attentive and appreciative readers of his famous travel book, for example: and, not least, the devotion of a small number of people who have studied him sufficiently to succumb, even after the interval of a century, to the charm which was irresistible to his contemporaries.

[1] They were bequeathed to the British Museum on the death of his daughter Darea Curzon, Baroness Zouche, in 1917, and are divided between the Departments of Manuscripts (Add. MSS. 39583–671) and of Oriental Printed Books and Manuscripts (Oriental MSS. 8729–855). The greater part of his printed books were sold at Sotheby's on 9 Nov. 1920.

VI *Walter Sneyd ◇ his drawings ◇ the Canonici purchase ◇ meets Madden ◇ Phillipps prints catalogue of his MSS. ◇ accessions ◇ gift from Duke of Hamilton ◇ inherits Keele ◇ correspondence ◇ dispersal of Sneyd's library*

PROFESSOR FRANCIS WORMALD, discussing with me on several occasions the plan of this book, expressed a desire to know more about Walter Sneyd,[1] the exceptional quality of some of whose illuminated manuscripts had long ago aroused his interest in a collector of rare discrimination. One would have wished that Sneyd's letters to Curzon had survived, but, if they have done so, I have failed to trace them. One amusing memento of their friendship, however, which throws light on Sneyd, came to my notice ten years ago, when Messrs. Peter Murray Hill offered an album of drawings for sale. This was secured by cable by the late Professor William A. Jackson of Harvard.[2] The drawings are nearly all by Sneyd, who sent them to Curzon: and the latter mounted them in the album. Sneyd was obviously a competent artist in a lively humorous vein. There are sketches of the friends as undergraduates, with other contemporaries at Christ Church, such as Hugh Cholmondeley and Lord de Tabley: and when they were in their early twenties, Curzon on the threshold of a diplomatic career and Sneyd just ordained, the artist drew a prophetic picture of them both in 1880. 'This snuff', says Curzon in the caption, 'was given me by the grand Signior when I was ambassador at Constantinople.' 'Ay?' replies the truly venerable cleric, 'That was in 1868, the same year that I was translated from

[1] Walter Sneyd, b. 1809, 2nd son of Walter Sneyd, d. 1829, of Keele, Staffs.; educ. Westminster and Christ Church, matric. 1827, B.A. 1831, M.A. 1834; ordained deacon 1834, curate of Baginton, Coventry, for a year, ordained priest 1835; lived at Denton House, Wheatley, Oxon., 1839–70; in 1856 m. his cousin Henrietta, who d. 1913, daughter of Richard Malone Sneyd; in 1870 inherited Keele Hall from his brother; died 1888.

[2] The album is Houghton Library bMS. Eng. 1129. Professor Jackson was good enough to send me information about it, and I am also indebted to his successor, Mr. William H. Bond, for further help and for permission to reproduce two of the drawings.

Worcester to the Archbishoprick.' There is an elaborate invitation of 1836, with the note 'Nicholas Jarry scribebat 1658'; a splendid picture of Curzon being tempted into extravagance by Payne and Foss (Plate 12); a representation of him 'picking up' a Caxton (*The Lyf of St. Catherine*) for a small sum; and a record of both friends meeting 'after their return from foreign travel in search of antient manuscripts' (Plate 14), Curzon wearing a tenth-century Gospels and Sneyd a fourteenth-century copy of the *Grands croniques de France*. These private pictorial jokes hardly bear translation into words, but I mention them to demonstrate that although Sneyd remains the more shadowy figure of the two, the gaiety was not all on Curzon's side. There is indeed other evidence of Sneyd's talents as both humorist and draughtsman. In 1829, when he was twenty, there appeared a quarto volume entitled *Portraits of the Spruggins Family, arranged by Richard Sucklethumkin Spruggins, Esq.* The lack of an imprint suggests private publication. The volume contains forty-four lithographic caricatures, all but three signed with Sneyd's initials, and an accompanying text of occasionally inspired absurdity.[1]

Sneyd, like Curzon, seems to have collected books as an undergraduate, but the evidence for the early years is scanty. In August 1833 we find a record of him buying books from De Bure in Paris, and already the tendency towards French and Italian literature, which together with medieval manuscripts became the main feature of the Sneyd Library, can be observed. It is possible that this bent towards Italian studies was derived from the books in the family library.[2] A catalogue is extant of the books at Keele in 1862, in the time of the occupation of the house by Sneyd's elder brother Ralph, and at that date the library contained a good many Italian books of the sixteenth century; but whether they formed part of the books among which Walter Sneyd grew up or were collected later by Ralph I do not

[1] The work has been attributed to Frances, Countess of Morley, but a note in the Bodleian copy is conclusive evidence of Sneyd's authorship (see *Bodleian Library Record*, viii. 3 (Feb. 1969), pp. 163–4). I am grateful to Mr. D. G. Neill for information on this subject. Sneyd's own copy of the book is in the library of the University of Keele.

[2] Mr. N. R. Ker has pointed out to me that the Sneyd family bred bibliophiles long before the nineteenth century, and that Ralph Sneyd, D.C.L., Prebendary of Bobenhull in the diocese of Lichfield, 1529–49, owned a number of manuscripts; see *Mediaeval and Renaissance Studies*, ii, 1950, p. 150, n. 3.

know. At all events his appetite for Italian literature and history must have grown rapidly. For in 1833 he began a negotiation of a size from which many very young collectors might have shrunk: the purchase of the residue of the Canonici manuscripts.

Matteo Luigi Canonici (1727–1805), a Venetian Jesuit, owned about 3,550 manuscripts, quite apart from a considerable collection of printed books, especially Bibles. Canonici died intestate and his collections passed into the possession of his brother, who himself died a year later. To the share of one of the brother's heirs, Giovanni Perisinotti, fell the manuscripts, and far the most important section of them, about 2,045 in number, was purchased by the Bodleian Library in 1817 for £5,444.[1] A few other manuscripts from the same source were consigned to Sotheby's on 26 February 1821, together with the manuscripts of Giovanni Saibante of Verona, by that indefatigable dealer and importer of books and works of art, the Abate Luigi Celotti; and, according to Sneyd, a further portion was sold to that great collector of manuscripts, Frederick North, 5th Earl of Guilford, a large part of whose collection passed into the library of Sir Thomas Phillipps. Perisinotti, however, had retained after these transactions over 1,000 manuscripts, including those relating to the history of Venice. In August 1833 Sneyd was in Venice and began to negotiate for them. Perisinotti employed as his agent a certain Simoni Occhi, and Sneyd, for his part, also worked through an intermediary, an Englishman resident in Venice, Thomas Holme; and the result of this multiplication of interested parties was that the transaction took two years to complete. The starting price was 749 Louis d'or, reduced a year later in August 1834 to 18,000 francs. On 29 September 1834 Occhi refused a request from Sneyd to divide the collection, and fixed a final and irreducible figure of 16,000 francs, about £650, an offer with which Sneyd apparently closed. Over a year elapsed, however, before the manuscripts reached England, owing to further negotiations over payment and over the means of circumventing a Venetian Government decree on the export of historical papers; and Sneyd does not seem to have received his purchase until after November 1835—261 manuscripts described

[1] See W. D. Macray, *Annals of the Bodleian Library*, 2nd edn., Oxford, 1890, pp. 299–301.

as 'Papal', 257 Venetian, and the rest listed under the title 'Miscellaneous', 1,029 in all.[1]

Doubtless it was a desire to recoup part of this substantial outlay that led Sneyd to consign a selection of the Canonici manuscripts to Sotheby's in 1836. He was certainly not discarding those unworthy of his collection, because the consignment included many of the most important and valuable items. If Sneyd's aim was to recover a major fraction of the cost price, the sale was a disastrous failure. Two hundred and seventy-eight lots, about 440 manuscripts in all, were offered on 25 June, and were knocked down for a beggarly £275. 6*s.* 0*d.*: but this was not the worst. Twenty of the most important lots failed to reach the reserve price and were bought in by Sneyd for a total of £232. 6*s.* 0*d.*, so that, taking into account the auctioneer's charges, he can scarcely have received anything at all for the 420 manuscripts which were sold.[2] It was, of course, the period of Dibdin's *Bibliophobia*, when prices were unnaturally depressed; and the stagnant market can scarcely have absorbed the large infusion of manuscripts from the Heber collection, sold in the previous February. Nevertheless, the fiasco must have been a bitter blow to the young collector's pocket and to his pride: and only in after years would he have thanked his stars that he had been wise enough to place protective reserves, and thus to retain some of the choicest treasures of the Sneyd Library. The most important of this group was lot 206, bought in for £45, a famous fourteenth-century geographical manuscript, Marino Sanuto's *Secreta fidelium Crucis, sive de recuperatione terrae sanctae libri tres*; this splendid book, decorated with maps, Sneyd was prevailed upon to sell to the British Museum in 1866 for £210.[3] Similarly Sneyd bought in for £25 lot 141, the richly decorated *Officium B.V.M.*, written in 1485 by Antonio Sinibaldi, for which Sir Sydney Cockerell gave £610 on behalf of Henry Yates Thompson at the Sneyd sale at Sotheby's in December 1903:[4] and for only £7. 10*s.* 0*d.* he retained lot 40, the Venetian

[1] Some correspondence relating to this transaction is in the Sneyd papers in Keele University Library, in S 26 (Library Papers), and the related catalogue is in S 167.

[2] Sneyd's copy of the sale catalogue, with some annotation, is also at Keele.

[3] B.M. Add. MS. 27376.

[4] B.M. Yates Thompson MS. 23.

Il Fiore di battaglia, with 124 miniatures of figures fencing, which is now Pierpont Morgan Library MS. 383.

Sneyd had met Sir Frederic Madden for the first time three weeks before the sale of June 1836. 'The Hon. Robt. Curzon Junior and his friend Mr Sneyd called on me', the Keeper of Manuscripts recorded in his journal on 1 June.

> The former I have already noticed (the 8th May) as an ardent collector of Mss. and the latter is not in this respect inferior, since he purchased above a thousand vols. of the *Canonici* collection, subsequent to the sale of part of that collection to the Bodleian Library. Among the Mss. then bought he told me was a bundle of fragments of old French Romances etc. and on my questioning him further, I discovered to my great surprise that among them was a portion (the conclusion) of the Metrical Romance of Tristan and Iseult, the existence of which was unknown to Michel, the recent Editor of the other fragments of this Romance. Mr Sneyd promised to bring it to the Museum, and allow me to make a copy of it for publication. The same gentleman told me he had purchased from Rodd the bookseller for 5. 5. 0 the identical *κοντακιον* described by Montfaucon in his Bibliotheca Bibl[iothecarum manuscriptorum],[1] as belonging to Baron Crassier, and had succeeded in decyphering the rubric, which according to Montfaucon could not be read, by which it was proved that the roll in question was executed for the Empress Eudocia in the year . . .[2]

Madden was obviously impressed by the young man's learning and acumen: and so was Sir Thomas Phillipps, whom Sneyd visited for a week in October 1837. Phillipps at once arranged to print a list of Sneyd's manuscripts in his *Catalogus Manuscriptorum Magnae Britanniae*, which he was planning at that time, and in due course they appeared in that rare work.[3]

Fifteen Greek manuscripts come first, headed by the Empress Eudocia's illuminated roll, which Sneyd afterwards described more fully for the Philobiblon Society.[4] A handful of Hebrew, Syriac, Arabic, Turkish, and Persian manuscripts follow. Numbers 23–34 are French, including a manuscript written by Jarry (No. 32), for whose work both Curzon and Sneyd had great admiration. The

[1] i, 1739, pp. 603–4.
[2] Bodleian MS. Eng. hist. c. 151, pp. 155–6.
[3] Pars I, Middle Hill, 1850, pp. 12–16, 13 *bis*–16 *bis*, 17–24, 46–55.
[4] *Miscellanies*, ii (1855–6).

Latin group (Nos. 35–117) opens with the celebrated Marino Sanuto. There was also a fourteenth-century Apocalypse with other texts (No. 51), with numerous full-page miniatures, and a respectable showing of fifteenth-century classical texts; but the great bulk of the collection consisted of Italian manuscripts from the fifteenth century onwards.

Very extensive purchases of printed books were made in Italy in 1839, mostly, it would appear from one of Sneyd's notebooks, at Florence, and the few small pieces of literary work with which the collector was concerned are mainly devoted to Italian subjects. In 1846 and 1847, for example, we find correspondence with John Holmes of the British Museum and with Albert Way of the Society of Antiquaries over Volume XXXVII of the Camden Society's publications, a translation by Sneyd's sister, Charlotte, of one of the Canonici manuscripts, a Venetian ambassador's account of England, written about 1500. Sneyd's contributions to the Philobiblon Society's *Miscellanies* are for the most part of a like nature, editions of short historical letters and papers selected from the same source.[1] It was doubtless a similarity of interest and fellow membership of the Philobiblon Society which brought Sneyd into correspondence with Edward Cheney,[2] one of the two Cheney brothers who were for many years prominent among British residents in Rome, and himself a considerable collector, whose fine library came under the hammer at Sotheby's on 25 June 1886.

Sneyd's collection, however, also embraced French books. The papers at Keele include a manuscript 'List of some Rare and Ancient Books at Denton House, Oxon.',[3] drawn up in 1847. Like many such catalogues undertaken by collectors, the project did not get very far: there are, in fact, only fifty-three entries, all of 'Black Letter French Books', printed between 1477 and 1540. But the range and quality are impressive. The collection includes the first undated Lyons edition of Honorat Bonner's *L'arbre de batailles*; the 1491 Lyons

[1] To vol. vii he contributed 'Letter from Queen Marie Antoinette to the Princess de Lamballe' and 'Relazione Della Regina di Suetia'.

[2] 1803–84, of Badger Hall, Shropshire, contributor of 'Remarks on the Illuminated Official Manuscripts of the Venetian Republic' to vol. xi of the *Miscellanies*. Monckton Milnes published an obituary of Edward Cheney in vol. xiv.

[3] In S 167.

edition of *La mer des histoires*; S. Augustine's *La cité de Dieu*, Abbeville 1486, the first volume only, but a great rarity; Antoine Verard's editions of Caesar, Quintus Curtius, Boccaccio, and Froissart; and a fine series of the illustrated early chronicles printed by Galliot du Pré and others, including such desirable books as *Les grandes croniques de Bretagne*, Caen 1518.

A few pieces of information about Sneyd during this period can be pieced together from his letters to Sir Thomas Phillipps.[1] On 14 July 1842 he announced that he had purchased Denton House, which he had previously rented, and that his books were stowed away in closets while the builders altered the house. 'I have scarcely added anything to my collection during the last 3 or 4 years', he reported. Nine years later, however, on 8 December 1851, he sent Phillipps a supplementary list of manuscripts which he had acquired since the Baronet had printed the original catalogue of his collection. 'My last *lucky hit*', he added, 'was the purchase of a *Psalter*, a good specimen of the 13th Century, well-preserved, and with ten illuminations, figures, on a raised bright gold ground, of which the first leaf nearly covers the page—it is a small 4to and I got it, very cheap, at a sale at Putticks in Piccadilly, last week.'[2] He went on to complain that manuscripts of this class were in general now beyond his means. 'Of old printed books', he ended, 'I still go on picking up a few every year and seek especially for French Black-letter books, and those with early woodcuts.'

The star item of Sneyd's collection, however, was acquired not by purchase but as a gift. The Marquess of Douglas was Sneyd's contemporary at Christ Church and their friendship endured until the former's death in 1863. The Marquess became the 11th Duke of Hamilton in 1852, and Sneyd spent Christmas of 1853 at Hamilton Palace, where he passed many hours engrossed with the manuscript treasures collected by the 10th Duke, or acquired through his wife, William Beckford's second daughter. Ruskin was a fellow guest and recorded in his diary on 22 December how he and the Duke spent the whole evening looking over the manuscripts with 'another missal

[1] In the Phillipps Correspondence in the Bodleian.

[2] Now Fitzwilliam Museum, McClean MS. 41.

admirer, Mr. Sneyd'. 'Nobody but the Duke and Duchess and we two bibliomanists at dinner', he added. 'House much too stately for my mind, though perfectly warm and comfortable, but five servants waiting on four people are a nuisance.' I have printed elsewhere the rapturous account of Hamilton and its treasures which he sent to Phillipps.[1] In 1856 Sneyd returned for a second visit. The 11th Duke took a considerable interest in the manuscripts inherited from his father, and Ruskin had noted with pleasure how well he cared for them, which makes the more generous the Duke's gift to Sneyd of a magnificent Flemish volume of the thirteenth century, a text of the Song of Songs, Proverbs, and Ecclesiastes, decorated with no less than 267 miniatures, 45 of them full-page. 'I congratulate you very much on the Duke of Hamilton's very Ducal present', wrote Curzon on 5 August, 1856, '. . . of its size and kind, I think the finest book I ever saw . . . One does not meet with such little tomes as that nowadays, nor indeed with presents of that sort of value and interest. Douglas is a generous fellow'; and he went on to recall how the Marquess had given him a set of studs as an undergraduate which he had worn for the last twenty-five years. 'Except my natural follies and shortcomings', he concluded characteristically, 'there is nothing that I have had so constantly about me as these little studs.'[2]

The Duke's noble gift to Sneyd was lot 513 in the sale of his library at Sotheby's on 16 December 1903, and it realized £2,500, well over twice the price of any other item. Bernard Quaritch, the purchaser, commissioned and printed a full description of the manuscript by M. R. James.[3] Plates were also made, illustrating 24 of the miniatures, but they seem never to have been issued; for the volume was sold almost at once to one of the French Rothschilds, I think to Baron Henri, although at the time of writing I have failed to ascertain its present whereabouts. I believe that it was one of the art treasures confiscated by the Einsatzgruppe Rosenberg and removed to Germany during the Second World War, and it is a melancholy

[1] *Phillipps Studies*, iv, 1956, pp. 95–6.

[2] Fraser No. 260.

[3] *Description of an illuminated MS. of the XIIIth century* (*Cantica Canticorum, Proverbia et Ecclesiastes cum aliis descripta*) *in the possession of B. Quaritch*, 8°, [1904].

coincidence that the only possibly comparable manuscript which M. R. James could cite was the *Hortus Deliciarum* of Herrade von Landsperg, destroyed by German shells in the siege of Strasbourg in 1870. Professor Wormald, however, who fortunately owns a complete set of photographs of the miniatures, tells me that James's parallel is not in fact very close, and that he knows of nothing which can be compared with Sneyd's manuscript, with its long series of mystical miniatures relating to the cult of the Virgin.

Sneyd's marriage in 1856, and a growing family, strained his financial resources to a degree which led him to tell Curzon that he feared that his books would have to be sold. The latter hastened to dissuade his friend. 'As to your selling your Gimcracks', he wrote on 13 January 1863, 'the very idea makes me feel alarmed. Why, what is life without Gimcracks, how can a man or at least an Abbot live without illegible manuscripts and incomprehensible editiones principes? I can understand going without breeches, but to give up one's Breeches Bible is what no fellow can stand or understand.'[1] Although hard-pressed for funds himself, he offered Sneyd a loan of £500, if it would avert such a calamity. The threat of the sale was averted, and seven years later, on the death of his elder brother, Sneyd inherited an ample fortune and the great house at Keele, where Curzon first visited him at the end of October 1870.

One of Walter Sneyd's most agreeable tasks was the rearranging of his books from Denton in the handsome library fitted out by Salvin for his brother. The books already in the house were by no means negligible; there was a large general library of standard works, and, as we have stated, a number of early Italian books, not to mention a few highly desirable items, such as the *editio princeps* of Homer.[2] In fact the collection was not at all suitable for instantaneous gift to the Working Man's Institute at Newcastle-under-Lyme, as Curzon light-heartedly proposed. The amalgamation of the two libraries led to a sale at Sotheby's on 19 March 1873 of 231 lots, mostly of standard sets which were doubtless duplicates, though one wonders

[1] Fraser No. 332.

[2] See the 'Catalogue of the Library of Ralph Sneyd Esq. at Keele Hall, 1862', manuscript in 2 vols., in S 167.

what made Sneyd discard lot 154, a small collection of quarto plays of the sixteen-thirties. At Keele the removal of financial stringency led to a considerable expansion of Walter Sneyd's book-collecting activities, and, according to an inventory, taken after his death in 1888, his collection had overflowed from the library itself and had invaded the entrance hall, staircase, organ-gallery, the old dining-room, and one of the bedrooms.

The importance of Sneyd's collection of manuscripts was underlined in 1872, when it received attention from the Historical Manuscripts Commission.[1] The great majority of the manuscripts, being Italian, were of course outside the scope of the Commission's interests, but a score of Canonici manuscripts which relate to English history are listed, including several important accounts of the Kingdom by Italian Ambassadors. Besides these the Commissioners' inspector enlarged on the importance of Sneyd's collection of original letters and documents from the sixteenth century onwards, among them autograph letters of Queen Elizabeth, Mary Queen of Scots, James V of Scotland, Charles I and II, William III, and other royal correspondents. These, with another volume of historical letters of the seventeenth century, are calendared in full, and similar series of French, Italian, and Spanish royal letters are briefly mentioned. A handful of medieval manuscripts are described; among them a tenth-century glossed Epistles of St. Paul and other texts from St. Augustine's, Canterbury,[2] and a fifteenth-century English version of Sir John Mandeville's *Travels*. The inspector also noted the presence in the library of the first edition of Johnson's *Dictionary*, profusely annotated by the author in preparation for the fourth edition of 1773.[3]

The correspondence which still survives at Keele relating to books and manuscripts, the letters from Curzon excepted, is disappointing both in bulk and interest. There are some letters from Peyton Blakiston, an old friend, a Fellow of Emmanuel College, Cambridge, who, having spent some years in the Church, lost his voice, studied

[1] *Third Report*, 1872, pp. 287–90.

[2] In the collection of the late Major J. R. Abbey.

[3] In the collection of the late Colonel Richard Gimbel, New York.

medicine, and became F.R.S. and an eminent physician. I have noted Sir Bernard Burke, Gladstone, and the second Baron De Tabley among the correspondents. There is a glimpse of two old friends in retirement in a letter from Henry Foss of 24 February 1863. His erstwhile partner Payne, he says, 'an idle fellow but very good natured', is wintering at Rome; in contrast, we hear of Foss's own activity and industry—serving his second term as Master of the Stationers' Company and busy with the administration of the Literary Fund. There are also a few letters from two considerable book-collectors, both members of the Philobiblon Society, with whom Sneyd kept on friendly terms throughout his life. One was William Stirling, later Sir William Stirling-Maxwell, celebrated for his researches on the artists of Spain, the owner of important works by Blake, and an extremely interesting library of emblem books;[1] works collected to illustrate the history of design; collections of proverbs; and other special subjects. The second was Evelyn Philip Shirley, the eminent antiquary and genealogist, Disraeli's Mr. Ardenne in *Lothair*, 'a man of ancient pedigree himself, who knew everybody else's'. Shirley formed two large libraries,[2] one at Lough Fea in Ireland and the other at Ettington, near Stratford-on-Avon, and in a letter of 14 February 1863 we hear of him fitting up the latter in a gallery seventy-six feet long at the top of the house, and bemoaning the snail's pace imposed on the operation by the effect of the agricultural depression upon his Irish rent-roll.

Sneyd's library did not long survive his death in 1888. Far the greater part of it, 866 lots, came under the hammer at Sotheby's on 16–19 December 1903, and realized £13,553. We have referred already to the sale of two of the most outstanding manuscripts, the *Officium B.V.M.* written by Antonio Sinibaldi (lot 556) and the noble Flemish picture book given to Sneyd by the Duke of Hamilton (lot 513). Many of the finest manuscripts were bought by Charles Fairfax Murray, and some of these passed from his collection into that of Dyson Perrins, in particular lot 516, the Beauvais

[1] Now in the library of the University of Glasgow.

[2] E. P. Shirley (1812–82) described part of his library in the rare *Catalogue of the Manuscripts at Ettington in Warwickshire, belonging to Evelyn Philip Shirley, Esquire, A.D. 1881*, 8°, 30 copies privately printed, 1881 and the *Catalogue of the Library at Lough Fea*, 1872.

Sacramentary of the late ninth century;[1] lot 555, the Adimari Hours, written at Florence about 1448;[2] and lot 557, a Bolognese Book of Hours illuminated by Taddeo Crivelli. These three manuscripts, which together realized the sum of £1,250 in 1903, realized £30,000 at the Dyson Perrins sales nearly half a century later. Perrins also acquired, not through Fairfax Murray, a number of other Sneyd manuscripts of lesser importance. A remarkable manuscript of the Apocalypse (lot 35), with the *Ars Moriendi* and some medical texts, containing no less than 292 miniatures, fetched £950, the second highest price in the sale, and is now in the Wellcome Historical Medical Museum; a tenth-century text of Pope Gregory's *Moralia in Jobum* was bought by Quaritch for £270, and was given in 1912 to the Grolier Club, New York, by Archer M. Huntington. The printed books in the sale must not detain us, though lots 170 and 171, Caxton's *Mirrour of the Worlde* and *The Golden Legende*, should not pass unmentioned.

Keele Hall, Salvin's massive neo-Elizabethan pile, laid a heavy burden on the resources of the Sneyd family. In the early years of the present century, bereft of its finest books, but still containing many art treasures, it was leased to the Grand Duke Michael. The twenties saw a further decline in the fortunes of the house; the pictures, plate, and other *objets d'art* provided four splendid sales for Messrs. Christie, while the remaining contents of the mansion were sold on the spot in 1928. In the meantime the residue of the library had been consigned to Messrs. Sotheby, who dispersed 934 lots for a further £11,957 in the sale which began on 28 November 1927. This sale contained many of Walter Sneyd's early woodcut books, but the star item was the author's annotated copy of Johnson's *Dictionary*, mentioned above, which realized £3,250. Only the French autograph letters and historical documents remained, and they too came under the hammer on 27 June 1932. Of these the most notable was lot 174, a moving letter from Marie Antoinette, in which she urged her close friend, the Princesse de Lamballe, not to return to Paris

[1] In 1968 it was in the collection of Peter and Irene Ludwig of Aachen; No. D 49 in exhibition 'Weltkunst aus Privatbesitz' at the Kunsthalle, Köln.

[2] Now in the Walters Art Gallery, Baltimore, MS. W 767.

owing to the dangerous state of public feeling[1]—a letter which denoted the end of an epoch and the sale of which marked the extinction of Walter Sneyd's noble library.

The collections of manuscripts formed by Sneyd and by his friend Curzon were products of the romantic medievalism which during their formative years as collectors manifested itself in the Eglinton Tournament, in ecclesiological controversy, and in cast-iron fan-vaulted conservatories. Both were highly personal collections and both fitted well into their antiquarian settings—at Parham a true one, at Keele an inspired pastiche.

The ornate library of the Sneyds was not destined to remain devoid of books for ever. The nineteen-fifties saw the beginnings of another—and a very different—library at Keele, that of the then University College of North Staffordshire, a collection of books more utilitarian, but one of which the cultivated and humane Walter Sneyd would certainly have approved, if he could have foreseen the day when the substantial provision which he and his brother had made for books was rendered totally inadequate by the astonishing windfall of Professor Sarolea's 200,000 volumes. But have *incunabula*, have chronicles, have romances entirely given place at Keele today to the journal and the textbook? I am glad to record that they have not, and that recently, with rare imagination, a modest gift was devoted to buying back one of Sneyd's manuscripts, an unpretentious thirteenth-century treatise on the Sacrament, but one which a former owner, Edward Johnston, rated highly for its good black Gothic hand: and there, together with Curzon's enchanting letters to his friend 'the Abbot of Denton', it remains as a memorial of a great nineteenth-century collector.

[1] See p. 112, n. 1.

VII *Bertram, 4th Earl of Ashburnham ⋄ his character ⋄ John Holmes ⋄ the 'Appendix' purchases ⋄ the Barrois transaction ⋄ acquisition of the Stowe manuscripts ⋄ inaccessibility of the Ashburnham manuscripts*

IN 1963 I devoted three Lyell lectures at Oxford to the collection of books and manuscripts formed by Bertram, 4th Earl of Ashburnham. A collector of printed books from his schooldays onwards, Ashburnham was middle-aged when he bought his first important manuscript in 1844. Five years later he had amassed more than 3,600 of them at a cost of over £22,000. His most sensational piece of bulk buying, the very large purchase in 1847 from the notorious Count Libri, I have written about at length elsewhere.[1] This was a highly dramatic episode in the history of book-collecting, and hardly less dramatic was the Thirty Years' War which Léopold Delisle waged to recover for his native France some of the treasures stolen by Libri from provincial libraries and sold to Lord Ashburnham: it is, however, not central to the subject of this book, and I shall not repeat any episodes from the Libri saga in this chapter. There remain to be considered two other large groups of manuscripts bought *en masse*, the Stowe and Barrois Collections, both acquired in 1849. And I shall study in more detail Ashburnham's individual purchases, which formed what he called the 'Appendix'; for in these the collector can be observed exercising choice, and they are thus a better touchstone of his taste.

The formation of this library is splendidly documented in the Ashburnham Papers deposited in the East Sussex County Record Office at Lewes,[2] and special help has been derived from the labours

[1] 'The Earl and the Thief', *Harvard Library Bulletin*, xvii. 1 (Jan. 1969), pp. 5–21; and 'The Triumph of Delisle; a Sequel', xvii. 3 (July 1969), pp. 279–90.

[2] See *The Ashburnham Archives: a Catalogue*, ed. Francis W. Steer, Lewes, 1958, particularly the Library Papers on pp. 51–4. I am much indebted to the 4th Earl's grandson, the late Mr. J. R. Bickersteth, and to Mr. Richard F. Dell for their help in making this archive available to me.

of the 4th Earl's wife, Katherine, who survived his death in 1878 by twelve years. She and her daughter constructed two elaborate volumes relating to the library. The first is an analysis of extant booksellers' accounts for purchases of books and manuscripts from 1827 to 1877,[1] and the second an interleaved and profusely annotated copy of the privately-printed *Catalogue . . . of the more rare and curious printed books . . . at Ashburnham Place*, 1864;[2] nor are sources for the study of this collection confined to the archives at Lewes.[3]

Lord Ashburnham (Plate 15) was born in 1797, and, as his grandson, Mr. J. R. Bickersteth, remarked to me, 'he would have fitted better into the century in which he was born than into the one in which he lived'. His proud and autocratic temperament bred legends of 'the old Bengal tiger at Ashburnham', who dismissed the Historical Manuscripts Commission as 'a society of ruffians who tamper with title-deeds'.[4] His control of the estates, which his family had owned at Battle, in Sussex, for 700 years, was patriarchal and despotic: nevertheless, I have it on Mr. Bickersteth's authority that, as a landlord, he was fair, even generous, and highly efficient. In the jargon of our day, however, his public image was cold, aloof, and unapproachable; and certainly the freemasonry of scholars and the social, clubbable, aspects of the fraternity of collectors were largely incomprehensible to him; nor is the faint commendation that 'he was by no means destitute of grim humour'[5] calculated to make us wish that we had known him.

Ashburnham was educated at Westminster School, and it is recorded that when he was a pupil there in 1814 he made his first purchase, a copy of the *Secretes* of Albertus Magnus for eighteen pence at Ginger's bookshop in Great College Street.[6] While he was at Westminster he already displayed his considerable talent as an

[1] Ashburnham MS. 4323.

[2] Ashburnham MS. 4336.

[3] After the sale of the contents of Ashburnham Place in 1953 the Bodleian acquired an annotated set of the privately-printed catalogues of manuscripts, and I myself bought the manuscript slip-catalogue of printed books, bound in 35 volumes, with much bibliographical annotation and a manuscript catalogue of the Bibles in the library.

[4] Augustus Hare, *The Story of My Life*, vi, 1900, p. 75.

[5] F. S. Ellis: article on Ashburnham in *Contributions towards a Dictionary of English Book-Collectors*, ed. Bernard Quaritch, x, 1897, pp. 1–11.

[6] W. Y. Fletcher, *English Book Collectors*, 1902, p. 382.

amateur artist: one of his etchings from this period is extant. With regard to his further education I can find no evidence in Cambridge to support the statement in *The Complete Peerage* that he proceeded to St. John's College. Indeed, diaries among the family papers suggest that he was travelling extensively in Europe as early as 1818, and a few years later he was ranging far beyond the normal confines of the Grand Tour, his itineraries between 1822 and 1825 embracing the Balkans, Russia, Asia Minor, and parts of Africa. This love of travel was reflected in the earliest book purchases of which we have record, the acquisition of a considerable number of voyages and similar works, bought from Payne and Foss in 1827. In the following year he was buying *incunabula* in Milan and early editions of Rabelais in Paris. In 1830 he succeeded to the Earldom, and to a family library which was substantial but not very remarkable, as an extant catalogue of 1821 testifies.[1] By the early eighteen-thirties the main pattern of his collecting could be distinguished, embracing *incunabula*, including finally a group of at least twenty-seven Caxtons, second only among those in private hands to the collection at Althorp, books on vellum of all periods, liturgies and Bibles, including two copies of the 42-line Bible, a fair showing of important books in English literature, and—a rather late development—chapbooks and early school-books. There were also superb author-collections of Chaucer and Dante, the completeness of the latter owing a good deal to the interest and assistance of Seymour Stocker Kirkup, the English artist and scholar who lived in Florence.

The acquisition of the major parts of the substantial collection of manuscripts, in contrast to the printed books, was concentrated over a very short period, barely 10 years, and was marked by three great purchases in bulk by which more than 3,600 manuscripts came into the collector's possession. In this field Lord Ashburnham had the good fortune to acquire the services of two able men, Thomas Rodd the younger and John Holmes. Rodd,[2] a bookseller of Great Newport Street, Long Acre, held the valuable British Museum agency. His sound knowledge of manuscripts and early printed books is widely attested, and to his reputation for absolute integrity there are many

[1] Ashburnham MS. 4320.

[2] See my *Phillipps Studies*, especially iii, 1954, p. 47.

witnesses. Grenville had a warm regard for him, Douce left him a legacy, and Sir Frederic Madden, a man notoriously reluctant to hand out compliments, paid him a glowing tribute. John Holmes had also been a bookseller, but at the time when he acted for Lord Ashburnham he was Senior Assistant in the Department of Manuscripts at the British Museum. He received his training with the firm of John Lepard, of 108 Strand, and in 1829 he compiled an elaborate catalogue of manuscripts for Lepard's successor at the same address, John Cochran.[1] He entered the British Museum in 1830, and was largely concerned with cataloguing the Arundel and Burney manuscripts. In 1843 he anonymously contributed a very interesting article to the *Quarterly Review* entitled 'Libraries and Catalogues'.[2] His letters to Lord Ashburnham, which are still preserved at Lewes,[3] begin on 9 October 1844, by which time he was obviously well established in the collector's confidence; and they extend to 1853, the year before his death. One hundred and twenty-one in number, they are full of interest; they document in detail not only the negotiations for the Libri and Barrois purchases, but also a large number of collections and individual manuscripts of note which came on to the market during the decade. Today the idea of a member of the British Museum staff actively seeking accessions for a private collector would strike us as rather odd: and on occasions there is evidence of an embarrassing conflict of loyalties. Holmes seems, however, to have made an honest attempt to serve both masters faithfully, and the head of his Department, Madden, who had no very high opinion of Holmes and who disliked private collectors, often kept secret from his assistant the Museum's intentions with regard to purchases, a wise precaution, because the national library and the Earl were, as we shall see, not infrequently in competition for the same articles.

[1] *A Catalogue of Manuscripts in different Languages . . . from the Twelfth to the Eighteenth Century, many of them upon vellum, and adorned with splendid illuminations: Now selling by John Cochran*, 8°, 1829. This catalogue, listing 650 items, with six illustrations and much learned annotation, issued in a cloth binding, was the most elaborate of its kind at that date: a similar catalogue, listing 691 manuscripts, was issued by Cochran in 1837.

[2] Vol. lxxii (May–Sept. 1843), pp. 1–25.

[3] Ashburnham MSS. 3564–622, 3648–709.

Lord Ashburnham's manuscripts, were, as is well known, divided into four groups, three of them, Libri, Barrois, and Stowe, being collections purchased *en bloc*, and the fourth, the Appendix, being the miscellaneous purchases made by Ashburnham between 1844 and 1877. We have already dealt with the Libri manuscripts; of the others we will trace the growth of the Appendix first.

Ashburnham formed substantial collections of objects of art—of coins, bronzes, Egyptian antiquities, carved gems, and especially of pictures, and it is interesting to note that his first recorded purchase of a group of important manuscripts was made not from a bookseller but from the well-known picture-dealer, Samuel Woodburn. On 23 April 1844 he paid Woodburn £150 for three manuscripts, two of them of considerable importance. One of them is now Pierpont Morgan Library MS. 191, a ninth-century Gospels, probably written at Tours, and the other Morgan MS. 641, a Gallican Missal of the eleventh century, with miniatures. The same year saw the purchase of two Chaucer manuscripts, one direct from Rodd and the other bought by him on commission at Benjamin Heywood Bright's sale,[1] as well as a few other manuscripts acquired from Henry Woodburn, Lilly, and Sams. A single manuscript only was bought in 1845, but accessions began in large numbers the year following, and in December 1846 the great Libri transaction began to be negotiated. Far the most important miscellaneous purchase of this year was made from the firm of Boone, to whom Ashburnham paid £350 on 12 September for what is now Pierpont Morgan MS. no. 1, the ninth-century Lindau Gospels, in the original binding of gold, silver, enamels, and jewels. Sir Frederic Madden heard of this acquisition from Rodd early in the following year, and recorded in his journal on 8 February 1847 the bookseller's glowing account of its exceptional quality and condition. 'This is very provoking', he added, 'as the Museum is sadly in want of some Mss. of this class.' In 1847 (apart from 1,923 manuscripts from Libri) thirty-three individual items were bought, including three of major importance. At the sale of the library of John Wilks, M.P., on 12 March Rodd bought on commission lot 442 for £210, the celebrated East Anglian

[1] See *Phillipps Studies*, iv, 1956, p. 15.

Psalter executed for the St. Omer family, now in the British Museum.[1] The collector acquired from Thorpe for £305 the fifteenth-century manuscript of forty-nine York miracle plays: this is now also in the British Museum,[2] which sent a commission of £500 for it when it appeared in the Ashburnham sale of 1899, and by one of those lucky accidents of the auction-room secured it for the very modest sum of £121. An important private purchase was also negotiated in 1847 with James Dennistoun of Dennistoun, who had brought back to England in 1838 the Book of Hours of Bonaparte Ghislieri of Bologna, which had been bought, with great difficulty, from the heirs of Cardinal Albani. This beautiful book, containing, along with much other decoration, a signed miniature by Amico Aspertini, greatly attracted Lord Ashburnham. John Holmes was involved in the affair, and the papers contain a dozen letters on the subject. Dennistoun was reluctant to sell, but finally, on 13 July 1847, he named what he described as being 'a fancy price' of 700 guineas, a very high figure for that date, but one which Lord Ashburnham accepted. This book formed part of Mrs. Yates Thompson's bequest to the British Museum.[3] I have found little evidence to support Bernard Quaritch's contention that Ashburnham 'could not compete with more openhanded buyers like the Earl of Crawford, Mr Henry Huth and Mr James Lenox of New York'. F. S. Ellis, indeed, states that by attempting to drive too hard a bargain with Sir John Tobin's heir he let slip the famous Bedford Book of Hours, but I have come upon no evidence which relates to this episode.

In 1848 over forty miscellaneous manuscripts were purchased, including a group of four Wycliffite Bibles from the Lea Wilson collection, bought by Ashburnham from Pickering, but these transactions pale into insignificance compared with those of the first half of 1849. These included the purchase of 702 Barrois manuscripts for £6,000 and 996 Stowe manuscripts for £8,000. With these two blocks we shall be dealing later. The Appendix, however, was also enriched by an exceptionally important manuscript at the beginning

[1] Add. MS. 39810.

[2] Add. MS. 35290.

[3] Yates Thompson MS. XCIII; his catalogue, iii, p. 145; his *Illustrations*, vi, pp. 79–88; B.M. Yates Thompson MS. 29.

of 1849, Beatus, *Super Apocalypsim*, written in Spain in the year 926 and decorated with ninety-three miniatures.[1] This noble and venerable volume is said to have been bought in Spain by Libri in 1847. It was in fact diverted from the British Museum by Libri, for Madden was negotiating for it through an agent named Leslie, and was deeply chagrined at his failure to secure it. Its origin is somewhat mysterious, for the provenance of the monastery of Volvacado, which Libri attached to it with a good deal of circumstantial detail, has been shown to be demonstrably false, and most recent scholarship assigns it to the monastery of San Salvador de Tavara. Holmes's letters to Ashburnham show that Libri brought this manuscript to London with him on his flight from France, that he offered it to Ashburnham through Holmes in April 1848, asking the peer to propose a price for it. I have found no record of his negotiations with the purchaser, but there is a note in the Ashburnham papers that it was bought, through the agency of Boone, for £525.

Although no spectacular mass purchases ever occurred again, there continued to be a stream of individual manuscript accessions; and a handful of examples must suffice for the later growth of the Appendix. In the early fifties Ashburnham bought a substantial number of manuscripts from Boone's stock and also from Kerslake, the Bristol bookseller. There was heavy buying at the Utterson sale in 1852 and at the sales of Sir William Betham and Clifton Wintringham Loscombe, F.S.A., in 1854. At the latter £113 secured a fourteenth-century collection of historical texts, including Henry of Huntingdon,[2] and £152 a copy of Piers Plowman, with other poetical works;[3] and on 27 December 1854 Sotheran supplied a distinguished manuscript, the Duc de Berri's copy of *La Bible Historiale* of Petrus Comestor, decorated with seventy-two miniatures.[4] During the next five years purchases of manuscripts tended to dwindle, with a revival in 1861, when several commissions were executed for the collector at the Savile, Tenison, and Dering sales. In 1862 Ashburnham bought a group of ten Greek manuscripts from Quaritch. These had been the property of the Earl of Aberdeen and had been included

[1] Pierpont Morgan MS. 644.

[2] Henry E. Huntington Library, MS. 1345.

[3] Ibid., MS. 128.

[4] Walters Art Gallery, Baltimore, MS. 501.

in the sale of the contents of his house in Argyle Place. Quaritch charged Ashburnham £20 apiece for them, and 'his lordship was so pleased with his bargain', the bookseller wrote later, 'that he made me a very acceptable present of game'. Of greater importance in this year were the commissions executed by Stewart at the most celebrated of the Libri sales, which began at Sotheby's on 25 July 1862, and at which Ashburnham laid out £520 for three French romances and a Dante manuscript. Two other purchases are worth singling out for mention. In February 1872 he bought at Sotheby's for £150 the fourteenth-century cartulary of the Benedictine Priory of Spalding,[1] a prize which would doubtless have escaped him, had not Sir Thomas Phillipps, that monopolist of cartularies, been on his death-bed. Finally, in 1877, the year before his death, he bought the most expensive single manuscript of his career, though by no means the most valuable by modern standards. He paid Ellis £1,750 for a magnificent manuscript of Wycliffe's Bible,[2] complete and in perfect condition; he already owned more than a dozen Wycliffite versions of the Scriptures, but, as he told the vendor, he had searched all his life for one in such condition.

This was the last manuscript to be added to the Appendix, which comprised a total of 254 items, acquired at a cost of about £13,200. In 1861 Ashburnham privately printed a catalogue of the first 203, and additional sheets carried the printed descriptions up to No. CCXXIV, acquired in 1863. Accessions after that were undescribed in print at the collector's death.

So much for the Appendix. There remain the Barrois and Stowe groups, acquired in that order. Jean-Baptiste-Joseph Barrois was born at Lille in 1784. His political career need not concern us here, but he had a modest niche in public life. He was elected deputy for Lille in 1824, and on the fall of the Bourbons took refuge in Belgium. He was an antiquary and scholar of not negligible attainments. In 1830 he published a series of fifteenth-century catalogues of old French royal collections, under the title *Bibliothèque Prototypographique*; he edited a number of early texts and wrote a volume of Carolingian

[1] B.M. Add. MS. 35296.

[2] Lot 177 in Sotheby's sale of 1 May 1899, at which Quaritch again paid £1,750 for it.

studies,[1] which was published in 1846 and found little favour among professional palaeographers. He died at Livry-sur-Seine on 21 July 1855. He was a very active collector of manuscripts and made purchases from English sources as well as from French. He owned, for example, a number of manuscripts from the Guilford, Hanrott, and Heber collections, but naturally the great French dispersals formed the source of many of his finest accessions, La Vallière, MacCarthy, Boutourlin, and especially the Pithou Collection, sold in 1837. I do not know whether there was any truth in a story told by Libri to Holmes, and repeated by Holmes to Lord Ashburnham in a letter of 20 April 1848, but I give it for what it is worth. 'M. Barrois', Libri had said, 'laid the foundation of his fine collection by seeing at a gold-beater's in Paris an immense number of mss. on vellum without their covers. The man told him that he had bought the Library at Lille at so much per lb. weight. It ended in M. Barrois giving the gold-beater a considerable advance on each lb. weight and buying the whole. The weight of mss. was so great that M. Barrois paid 30,000 francs.' Unfortunately, some of the 700 or so manuscripts which Barrois acquired were derived, in Léopold Delisle's expressive term, 'from an impure source', a dealer who sold him nearly sixty manuscripts recently stolen from the Bibliothèque Royale. Delisle produces convincing evidence to show that Barrois was aware of the provenance of at least some of these books;[2] for several which had been in the library of Charles V were listed in his own *Bibliothèque Prototypographique*, and these were rebound by Barrois with Charles V's arms on the covers. Whether he or his impure source was responsible for other attempts to conceal the origins of the manuscripts we may never know, but several bore suspicious and significant mutilations, false inscriptions, and new bindings.

There is little doubt that it was the scandal that followed Libri's exposure which prompted Barrois to sell his manuscripts abroad in 1848. The former's thefts from the Bibliothèque Royale were the subject of official investigation, and the knowledge that another

[1] *Éléments carlovingiens linguistiques et littéraires*, 4°, Paris, 1846.

[2] See his *Observations sur l'origine de plusieurs manuscrits de la Collection de M. Barrois*, 8°, Paris, 1866; and *Les Manuscrits du Comte d'Ashburnham: Rapport au Ministre de l'Instruction Publique*, 4°, Paris, 1883.

stolen cache from the same source rested on his own shelves must have been highly uncomfortable to Barrois. He placed the negotiations in the hands of his Parisian binder, P. Thompson, an Englishman, who lived at 76 Rue d'Anjou. As early as April 1848 Libri had suggested to Holmes that the Barrois manuscripts might come on to the market, and rumours to that effect seem to have circulated briskly round the trade. Rodd went to France to investigate, and on 15 July he called on Madden at the British Museum to report on his visit.[1] Barrois had, he said, at first asked £12,000, whereas Rodd's own estimate of the value of the collection—to a bookseller, for resale—was £4,500, and he had offered this sum. Barrois had countered by dropping his price to £6,000, payable within ten years, or secured by an annuity on his life. Rodd was not disposed to close with this offer on his own behalf, but submitted it to Madden, suggesting that, if the Museum were the purchaser, he should receive five per cent as intermediary. Madden worked over Rodd's list of the principal manuscripts, with his estimates of their value, and decided that the acquisition would be a desirable one. Accordingly he drew up a report on the subject for submission to the Trustees. 'I do not think there is the least chance of their accepting the offer', he wrote in his journal, 'or of applying to the Treasury for money, but Forshall thinks I should do right in placing the matter before them, so that they may judge for themselves.' If the Trustees declined the manuscripts, Madden recorded, it was Rodd's intention to approach Lord Ashburnham.

The Trustees met on 22 July, and a week later Madden, who was on holiday, received from Forshall a copy of the minute on his application. After setting out the nature of the collection and Madden's recommendation for its purchase, the minute continued:

Sir Frederic Madden expressed his opinion that the real reputation and riches of a national library consisted of its Ms. Collections, and gave a detailed account of the grants that had been made at various times for the purchases of Collections of Mss, and urged on the Trustees the advantage of buying entire Collections. Sir Frederic Madden also gave a list of some of the most valuable Mss. in the present Collection, and

[1] Bodl. MS. Eng. hist. c. 161, pp. 194–202.

added that the sum of £5000, if paid shortly, would probably be accepted by the proprietor.

Upon this Report the Trustees made no Order.

'Just what I expected,' commented Madden, 'so I am not disappointed, however I may say, *Liberavi animam meam*, and the blame of refusal rests with the Trustees.'[1]

Rodd was duly informed of this decision, and on 3 August Holmes, on his behalf, made the same proposal to Ashburnham. The bookseller stipulated secrecy, and his commission of five per cent, if the purchase were made. In a reply to Holmes of 5 August the Earl repudiated Rodd's pledge of confidence, for he had already been aware that the manuscripts were on the market. If Barrois wished to sell them to him, he said, there would doubtless be some direct approach. It is not clear to me why Ashburnham did not make use of Rodd's services, for he had proved his reliability in the Libri negotiation; and our full understanding is hampered by the fact that the papers at Lewes contain apparently only selected letters on this episode. By October 1848 the size of Rodd's offer seems to have been generally known in the trade. James Clyde of 88 Newman Street, a relatively minor bookseller, wrote to Ashburnham offering the collection for £6,000, stating that £4,500 from another bookseller had recently been refused: and in November A. Asher of 10 Bedford Street also solicited Ashburnham to employ him as agent in the matter.

The collector already had some idea of the nature of the manuscripts from Holmes, to whom Libri had given information on the subject. He was seriously interested, and in November he was in touch with Thompson himself, who sent him an inadequate account of a few of the manuscripts and urged their acquisition. There was talk of Holmes going to France straight away, but attempts were made to get more details from Thompson first. Barrois, it emerged from a letter from Thompson of 1 December, was ill and could not himself produce a detailed catalogue, but on 21 December Thompson wrote to say that he had visited Livry, where Barrois had handed him the key to his library and allowed him to make notes as he

[1] Bodl. MS. Eng. hist. c. 161, pp. 213–14.

wished. Thompson enclosed further particulars of several manuscripts about which Ashburnham had inquired, especially two of the eighth century and a fourteenth-century Dante. Barrois, so Thompson volunteered, 'did not receive M. Libri', but had lent him a manuscript for study through a third party. The collections included Anglo-Saxon manuscripts, he added, and also Greek; and Barrois would only contemplate the sale *en bloc*. Thompson was clearly no expert in manuscripts, and if Ashburnham was to get an authoritative opinion on the collection he must obviously dispatch his own agent to France: and accordingly Holmes went there on his behalf in February 1849. From Paris he wrote two enthusiastic letters. The general condition of the collection was fine, he said, and the French romances unrivalled. The deal was closed, the £6,000 paid, and the manuscripts dispatched on 8 March. The transaction was satisfactory to all parties except Thompson, whom Barrois refused even his expenses as an agent in the matter, and Ashburnham rewarded with a *pourboire* of £20.

Of the 702 manuscripts bought on this occasion far the largest part were French. The collection was exceptionally strong in French medieval poetry and romances, and, as one would expect, rich in manuscripts decorated with miniatures. A number of the grandest books of this class from the Barrois Collection are now in the Pierpont Morgan Library; Morgan MS. 212, for example, the French version of Orosius's history, with 391 miniatures in grisaille; or Morgan MSS. 672–5, a French Voragine with 143 miniatures: Barrois had scores of such books. Many had been lavishly rebound by Barrois himself, but the collection also included some fine medieval bindings, seven of them decorated with ivories. There was also a handful of very early books, some Latin classics, and a group of manuscripts which related to the history of the Low Countries. Ashburnham printed a catalogue of them all, compiled by Holmes.[1] It was not until he gave a finely bound set of his catalogues to Paul Meyer in 1865 that the French authorities awoke to the fact that the Barrois group, as well as the Libri, contained stolen treasures: and

[1] *Catalogue of the Manuscripts at Ashburnham Place, Part the Second, Comprising a Collection formed by Mons. J. Barrois*, 4°, n.d.

in the event, after years of haggling, 166 items from the Libri and Barrois collections were ultimately recovered by the Bibliothèque Nationale in 1888.[1] The rest of the Barrois manuscripts were sold at Sotheby's in June 1901 for £33,217.

The main outline of the transaction in which Ashburnham acquired the Stowe manuscripts is well known,[2] but a few touches can be added to our knowledge of the British Museum's failure from Madden's journals.[3] The Stowe collection itself, having been the subject of three printed catalogues,[4] requires only the most summary description here. Formed by the 1st Duke of Buckingham and Chandos, it owed its fame largely to the absorption of two earlier collections, that of Thomas Astle, Keeper of the Tower Record Office, and that of Charles O'Conor of Balnagare. Astle's manuscripts were exceptionally important, containing forty-two Anglo-Saxon charters, King Alfred's Psalter, the eleventh-century register of Hyde Abbey, other cartularies, chronicles, and wardrobe books, many from the earlier accumulations of Sir Roger Twysden, John Anstis, and Astle's father-in-law, Philip Morant, the historian of Essex. In addition to the Astle and O'Conor manuscripts, the latter nearly all relating to Ireland, the Duke had made a number of other purchases, notably the papers of Arthur Capell, 1st Earl of Buckingham, and correspondence of the 1st Duke of Marlborough.

When financial ruin overtook the 2nd Duke, and the art treasures of Stowe were sold in August 1848, it was natural that the fate of this famous collection of manuscripts should have excited wide public speculation. Madden worked through the printed catalogue of 1818 and recorded in his journal on 21 September his estimate of the collection's value. His figure, £8,360, turned out to be extremely near the mark. Moreover, he reached an understanding with the

[1] See *Bibliothèque Nationale: Catalogue des manuscrits des fonds Libri et Barrois*, par Léopold Delisle, 8°, Paris, 1888; and *Liste des manuscrits de la collection Barrois récemment acquis pour la Bibliothèque Nationale*, par Henri Omont, 8°, Paris, 1901.

[2] S. De Ricci, *English Collectors of Books and Manuscripts*, Cambridge, 1930, p. 131.

[3] Bodl. MS. Eng. hist. c. 162, *passim*, especially pp. 129–40.

[4] Charles O'Conor, *Bibliotheca manuscripta Stowensis*, 2 vols., 4°, Buckingham, 1818–19; *Catalogue of the important Collection of Manuscripts from Stowe, which will be sold by S. Leigh Sotheby & Co., on 11 June 1849* . . ., 8°, 1849; *Catalogue of the Stowe Manuscripts in the British Museum*, 2 vols., 8°, 1895–6.

Marquess of Chandos, acting for the Duke's creditors, that the British Museum should have the first refusal in the event of a sale. In January 1849 he appears to have brought the matter to the Trustees of the Museum, but at that time they were content to await developments and not to initiate any action. In February Sir Thomas Phillipps offered £6,000, which Lord Chandos refused, and a rumour of this offer reached Madden through Rodd. On the 27th of that month Madden saw at Sotheby's the proofs of a sale catalogue, 'drawn up by Mr Smith, the Duke's librarian, and very strangely arranged', for the creditors had by that time been persuaded that a sale by auction would be most advantageous; and it was duly fixed to begin on 11 June. In March Rodd reported the rumour that no sale would take place after all, since the Marquess of Breadalbane would find the purchase price and the manuscripts be retained in the family. 'If they are to be *locked up* for another century, I am sorry for it' was Madden's comment.

On 18 April matters came to a climax. On that date Madden met Rodd and Samuel Leigh Sotheby at the latter's auction rooms. There he heard for the first time that Ashburnham had made a firm offer of £7,000 in cash for the whole collection, and that Lord Chandos was disposed to accept. Sotheby had advised against the private sale for such a figure and urged Madden to write at once to Chandos on the subject. As Rodd and Madden walked home along the Strand together the bookseller unburdened himself. 'He complained much of Lord Ashburnham's conduct to himself, as overbearing and insolent, so that he had left off dealing with him' Madden recorded. 'This confirms what Lilly told me of his Lordship's conduct. I brought away two more copies of the sale catalogue (not yet published) as Lord A. has laid claim to the whole, in case he became the purchaser of the Mss!'

On his return to the Museum Madden lost no time in writing to Lord Chandos to remind him of his promise that the national library should have first refusal of the manuscripts. His Lordship's reply was received on 21 April. He had, he said, been in communication with Sir Robert Peel on the subject, and had already informed him that a substantial private offer had been made. He added that if the

Museum's Trustees would seriously entertain the proposition, he would name a price for the whole collection, probably from £8,000 to £10,000. Madden's journal then contains an account of the Trustees' meeting at which the decision was made, and at which the Keeper of the Department of Manuscripts merits our deepest sympathy.

A meeting of the Trustees took place today [21 April 1849], to which I was summoned. Lord Northampton was in the chair, and Sir R. Peel, Lord Cawdor, Lord Cadogan, Sir R. Inglis, Hallam, Hamilton, Macaulay, and many more were present. I read to them the passage in Lord Chandos's letter relative to the price, and a discussion then arose, as to the propriety of applying to the Government for the purchase of the whole, and the steps to be taken for further communication with Lord Chandos. The greater part of the Trustees present sat quite *silent*, and *not one* ventured openly to propose to buy *the whole*. On the other hand, Mr Macaulay, having looked at a copy of a catalogue laid on the table, declared loudly, that as the Grenville correspondence and the Junius letters had been withdrawn, the only interesting portion of the Collection (!) it was not advisable to apply to the Government for the purchase of Anglo-Saxon and Celtic Mss. however curious they might be!!! Here is a valuable Trustee! a literary Trustee! It was in vain I strove to show that the value and reputation of the Stowe Collection of Mss. did not rest upon some political chitchat of the Grenville family or on five letters of Junius,—I spoke to the deaf. Sir Robert Peel alone (and he from motives of *popularity*) suggested, that we should treat for the Irish Mss. separately, and although I told him plainly, I was certain no such proposition would be entertained by the creditors, yet the rest of the Trustees gave a silent acquiescence, & Sir R. Peel was requested to draw up a minute to that effect. I then made my bow, perfectly convinced in my own mind, that the Stowe Mss. would never enter the Museum walls.

On the day following Madden received Peel's minute and wrote at once to Lord Chandos in the terms agreed by the Trustees, adding on his own account an urgent request for a personal interview. On 24 April Lord Chandos called at the Museum, and, although he thought it most unlikely that the creditors would be willing to sell the Irish MSS. separately, he agreed to put the proposal to them. The price, he told Madden, had been definitely fixed at £8,000, and he gave a reassurance, unnecessary in Madden's case, that the only portions which had been withdrawn were some family legal papers, the letters of Junius, which had been mislaid, and the Grenville Correspondence, which contained many confidential matters relating to the living and the recently dead. Lord Ashburnham, Chandos stated, was the Museum's sole competitor.

The decision which Madden feared and expected was taken on the next day and conveyed to the Keeper of Manuscripts in two notes from Lord Chandos. The first merely stated that the creditors would not sell the Irish manuscripts alone: the second, marked *Private*, informed Madden that rather than wait for a decision from the Trustees and the Government, it had been decided to accept Lord Ashburnham's offer of £8,000 and close the negotiation: and in default of any realistic proposal from the Museum it is difficult to see that they could have acted otherwise. Thus the Stowe manuscripts, as Madden thought, passed out of the nation's reach. 'I really believe both the Trustees and the Government will be glad to get rid of them' was his bitter comment. It was not, of course, until 1883, after Madden's death, that after hard bargaining with the 5th Earl of Ashburnham the Museum acquired the Stowe collection for £45,000;[1] and the Irish section was then detached and placed on loan in Dublin in the custody of the Royal Irish Academy.

Lord Ashburnham's great collection of books and manuscripts cost him about £60,000, of which the printed books accounted for rather less than £23,000. To finance this large expenditure, much of it concentrated over a short period, the collector consigned to Christie's in 1850 a major part of the pictures which he had inherited. These had been brought together by the 2nd Earl (1724–1812), and were of a kind no longer fashionable in 1850 among English collectors. Indeed, the only buyer who seems to have bid energetically for them was the Marquess of Hertford, a connoisseur in whom eighteenth-century tastes still survived, and in the event nearly half the lots offered failed to reach their reserves and were bought in by the 4th Earl.[2]

[1] See the House of Commons Order Paper, 27 July 1883, *Ashburnham Manuscripts, Copy of Papers relating to the Purchase of the Stowe Collection by Her Majesty's Government.*

[2] See Sotheby's Introduction to their sale catalogue of 24 June 1953, when the first part of the residue of the paintings at Ashburnham Place came under the hammer.

Ashburnham's manuscripts were among the half dozen most important collections formed in this country. They had, however, little influence on the taste and connoisseurship of his day, because they were extremely inaccessible. It is a paradox that Lord Ashburnham, who printed and distributed catalogues of his manuscripts, was curiously reluctant to face the natural result of having publicized the immensely rich materials in his possession and to receive visits from inquiring scholars. 'His lordship is a dog in the manger', complained Madden, and there are many contemporary references in the same vein.[1] Mr. Bickersteth has pointed out to me that his grandfather's reputation for being inhospitable may have stemmed less from temperament than from his domestic circumstances. At Ashburnham Place the books and manuscripts were in two rooms, the large and small libraries. The former was the common sitting room of a numerous family and the latter Ashburnham's private study; a protracted visit from a stranger meant a good deal of domestic disruption. Nevertheless, it is on record that scholars were from time to time warmly received. 'My kind host', wrote Georg Heinrich Pertz to his wife on 15 July 1857, 'not only told me at once to make use of all his literary treasures, as much as I should like, but expressed at the same time the hope I would stay as long as necessary, as he himself remains here for two or three months longer, and should be glad to see me make the best use of his manuscripts.'[2]

In the context of visitors to Ashburnham Place, I would like to end this chapter by recounting an episode which illustrates well several facets of Ashburnham's character—his rather grudging permission to examine his manuscripts, his sharp reaction to an understandable and tentative inquiry about the possibility of the sale of part of them to Trinity College, Dublin, and his epistolary style, in which a downright snub is blandly conveyed.

Dr. James Henthorn Todd, at the time of his meeting with Lord

1 See Ashburnham's frigid correspondence with Sir Thomas Phillipps in my *Phillipps Studies*, iv, 1956, pp. 27–8, and Dr. Waagen's bitter complaints at the unacceptable conditions proposed for his visit to Ashburnham Place in 1850 (*Treasures of Art in Great Britain*, iii, 1854, pp. 28–9).

2 *Autobiography and Letters of George Henry Pertz*, ed. by his wife, 8°, privately printed, n.d., p. 156.

Ashburnham, was President of the Royal Irish Academy, Senior Fellow of Trinity College, Dublin, and also Librarian of that great institution. During his tenure of office he greatly enriched the collections, especially in the field of Irish historical material, and when Lord Ashburnham carried off the Stowe manuscripts in 1849 it was natural enough that an application from Dr. Todd to inspect them should have followed. In particular he wished to collate the ancient Irish legal manuscript, 'The Book of Acaill'. In 1851 Lord Clarendon's influential aid was invoked, but it was not until May 1855 that Todd was received at Ashburnham Place. In addition to 'The Book of Acaill', Todd examined carefully the famous Stowe Missal (so-called—it is really a Sacramentary), and he read an account of it to the Royal Irish Academy in June 1856. I possess the copy of the offprint of this paper that Todd sent to his host,[1] not entirely tactfully, because it contains a number of imperfectly concealed asperities at the expense of what Todd called 'the noble possessor': and the noble possessor in his turn has pencilled in the margins some less than friendly remarks on Dr. Todd. In particular Todd wrote: 'Lord Ashburnham did not permit me to transcribe anything, and I was, therefore, forced to content myself with a careful perusal of the MS., comparing it as I read with Dr O'Conor's description of it.' Against this passage Lord Ashburnham has written: 'This is absolutely false. I did not very often interrupt the Doctor while he was here—but I never entered the MS Room without finding him with pen or pencil in his hand—& he certainly copied the Breton Laws—or told me that he did so.'

I think that the tartness of this interchange was occasioned by some correspondence which took place soon after Todd's departure from Ashburnham Place. During his visit Todd sounded his host on the possibility of selling the Irish manuscripts to Trinity College. What transpired in conversation we do not know, but at all events Todd was sufficiently persistent to write, on his return to Ireland, and make a formal offer. Lord Ashburnham's reply was characteristically frosty.

[1] 'On the Ancient Irish Missal, and its Silver Box, . . . now the Property of the Earl of Ashburnham', from the *Transactions of the Royal Irish Academy*, xxiii: *Antiquities*, 4°, Dublin, 1857.

Ashburnham Place
31 July [1855]

Reverend Sir,

It was far from my intention to 'hint' anything about disposing of my Irish Manuscripts, & I am sorry as well as surprised to find that you have misunderstood that which I cannot but think was stated in very plain terms.

I perfectly remember saying that I would not part with those Mss.—& I afterwards explained my meaning to be that I certainly would not sell them—but that for reasons of which you are not ignorant, I might be tempted to part with the Irish Mss., by way of exchange. I am still in the same mind: they are not for sale, & therefore I need make no remark upon your offer—if it be an offer—of £500 for them.

I have not, & never had, any more expectation than you have, of your being able to procure a Ms for which I would exchange my Irish collection. But since you have made me an offer, let me make one in return. If you will send me one of the finest Mss now in your possession—for instance the Book of Kells—I will tell you whether I will or will not give my Irish Mss for it.

This proposal may, on many accounts, be inadmissible—but I beg to say (I think not for the first time) that it is no more so than would be an offer of five times five hundred pounds for my collection of Irish Mss.

I am, Reverend Sir,
Your obedient servant
Ashburnham[1]

It is perhaps unnecessary to add that these frost-bitten seeds of negotiation did not germinate, let alone bear fruit.

[1] I owe the text of this letter, in the Library of Trinity College, Dublin, to the kindness of the Keeper of Manuscripts, Mr. William O'Sullivan.

VIII *Seroux d'Agincourt* ⬦ *Henry Shaw and Madden* ⬦ *decorative use of manuscripts* ⬦ *J. O. Westwood* ⬦ *Bastard d'Estang* ⬦ *R. S. Holford* ⬦ *the Alcuin Bible transaction* ⬦ *Dr. Waagen* ⬦ *John Ruskin*

IN 1823, nine years after the death of its author, appeared the final volume of a work which, in its recognition that all branches of the Fine Arts, both major and minor, are indivisible, gave a new impetus to the study of our subject. Jean-Baptiste Seroux d'Agincourt (1730–1814), cavalry officer turned art historian, devoted the last forty years of his life to the study of the arts from their decline in the final phase of the Roman Empire to their rebirth at the Renaissance. His great work, *Histoire de l'Art par les Monumens, depuis sa décadence au IVᵉ siècle jusqu'à son renouvellement au XVIᵉ*, appeared in Paris in six folio volumes between 1810 and 1823, and on its 325 plates were reproduced thousands of examples of architecture, sculpture, and painting. Many of the latter placed before the world for the first time examples of early Christian paintings from the catacombs, on which Seroux d'Agincourt was an expert, and especially miniatures from manuscripts. His aim was to record rather than to comment, and unfortunately many of the miniatures he reproduced were from manuscripts not precisely identified. His book, which was rare and costly, was not, I think, very influential in England until after its appearance in a three-volume translation in 1847. Nevertheless, Sir Frederic Madden, in a work which I am about to consider, knew it well and commended it, and quotes with approval the Frenchman's justification of the study of medieval miniatures.

'Miniature painting', he asserted, 'although a secondary branch of the art, may claim the merit of having contributed in a great measure to the reestablishment of painting on a grander scale, and also of having preserved by the beauty or *bizarrerie* of its designs many valuable works from destruction, which would else have perished, in common with other monuments less adorned.'

Madden's quotation comes from his Introduction to a book, the first of a long series important in the dissemination of taste for the Gothic, Henry Shaw's *Illuminated Ornaments selected from Manuscripts of the Middle Ages*, handsomely published by William Pickering in 1833. Shaw (1800–73), a professional architectural draughtsman and illuminator, developed his subject throughout his life in a row of publications which culminated in his *Handbook of the Art of Illumination as practised during the Middle Ages*, 1866. In his first book he was fortunate to secure Madden's collaboration, for the latter's account of the development of miniature painting is certainly the most sensible and coherent treatment of the subject written by that date.

Madden initially reviews the few previous works on the theme, and expresses relief that the Abbé Rive's *magnum opus* stopped short at its prospectus, since the engravings 'were so wretchedly and faithlessly executed, that no regret can be felt at the discontinuance of the Abbé's design'. Dibdin's enthusiastic outpourings are tactfully dismissed as 'tasteful selections with a running commentary, rather than a critical history of the progress of art'. D'Agincourt is praised, but with an important qualification.

> His work [comments Madden] is by no means complete, for, were his specimens always faithfully delineated, (which there is often reason to doubt) they are confined almost wholly to manuscripts executed by Greek and Italian artists, and afford only a casual and very unsatisfactory glimpse of the state of art in the greater portion of Europe. Great Britain, indeed, is wholly neglected, yet there are well-founded grounds for belief, that more considerable progress in design and colouring had been made during the tenth and eleventh centuries in England and France, than in Italy.

This observation, obvious to us today but then an unfamiliar idea, was not in fact Madden's own, and he cites in evidence a letter written by H. Y. Ottley to the antiquary John Gage, and printed by the latter in his long account of the Benedictional of St. Æthelwold contributed to *Archaeologia*.[1]

[1] xxiv (1832). This article of 117 pages, plus 32 plates, is the most extensive and elaborate account of an illuminated manuscript to be published at this date.

Madden begins his survey by tracing back to antiquity certain features, such as the marking of opening paragraphs in vermilion, the origin of the application of gold and silver leaf and of the sumptuous *codices purpurei*. The practice of writing whole manuscripts in gold letters is discussed, with examples. The Hiberno-Saxon school, already identified by Dr. Charles O'Conor in the first volume of his *Rerum Hibernicarum Scriptores*, Buckingham, 1814, gets for the first time its proper treatment in such a general survey, and the schools of illumination which grew up under the patronage of Charlemagne and Charles the Bald are accorded their true importance. In England the Winchester School is given a status equal or even superior to that of any Continental work of the period. The elaboration of capital letters in the twelfth century is noted. In the thirteenth Madden discerns a decline—'the art of illuminating, in some respects deteriorated, and endeavoured to supply in splendour what it lost in correctness of taste', and he calls in evidence the introduction of solid gold backgrounds; but the developments in Italy, associated with the names of Nicola Pisano, Cimabue, and Giotto, are seen as a revolution in design. English and French workmanship of the fourteenth century is extolled, with special reference to the Gorleston Psalter, then in the library of Lord Braybrooke; the first time, I believe, that that great manuscript was brought to the notice of the public. The fifteenth century is seen as a period when the art of painting 'made rapid strides towards the perfection it attained in the subsequent age', for Madden was not ahead of his contemporaries in regarding the sixteenth century—and Clovio in particular—as the age of the final triumph of the illuminator's art. As well as composing the Introduction, Madden had, of course, a hand in the selection of the manuscripts illustrated in this handsome book. They are drawn from two public collections, the British Museum and Bodleian, and four private ones, those of Ottley, Lord Braybrooke, Douce, and Hanrott.

Shaw's *Illuminated Ornaments*, 1833, began a vogue of picture-books of details of manuscripts which proliferated within two or three decades, when chromolithography made the reproduction of miniatures in colour a relatively cheap process. By the middle of the forties the practice of illumination at all levels was becoming a fashionable pursuit, and some splendid books catered for the growing public, such as Henry Noel Humphreys's *The Illuminated Books of the Middle Ages*, 1849, with fine chromolithographs by Owen Jones. Lower down the scale were a shelf-full of Grammars, Guides, Alphabets, Hints, Primers, Manuals, Lessons, and Handbooks for aspirant illuminators, a class numerous enough to support a magazine, *The Illuminator*, by 1861. Mr. Ruari McLean has been good enough to send a list of such works on his own shelves, and a glance at a few obvious subject-indexes has shown me how astonishingly numerous these works were. We cannot pursue the subject here, but this popular by-product of the awakening interest in the medieval miniature must not pass unrecorded.

Already in the 1820s the decorative qualities of illuminated manuscripts were being drawn upon by artists and architects. Mr. Nicolas Barker drew my attention to a portrait of Sir Thomas Dick Lauder, 7th Baronet (1784–1848), who was painted with his wife by William Nicholson in 1821.[1] The couple are in sixteenth-century costume and Sir Thomas is indicating to Lady Lauder a passage in a folio medieval manuscript propped open before him. This conception obviously owes much to the influence of the author of *Waverley*.

In the field of architecture I am indebted to Mr. Edward Croft-Murray for a most interesting reference in the unpublished second volume of his *Decorative Painting in England*. Throughout the century under review painted decoration in the Gothic manner was, of course, not uncommon, and Mr. Croft-Murray has collected together information on the significant examples; those at The Vyne, Lee Priory, and Arbury Hall (Warwickshire), among the most outstanding. At the end of our period, however, he has added an example quite unknown to me hitherto, the work of A. W. Pugin at Scarisbrick Hall, Lancashire, in 1837, where, far from stopping at the introduction of Gothic motifs, Pugin decorated the Red Drawing Room with copies of two medieval miniatures. The manuscript from which they were copied is, moreover, identifiable,

[1] In the collection of Sir George Dick Lauder, Edinburgh. I am grateful to the National Portrait Gallery for permission to examine a photograph of this picture.

a *Roman de la Rose* in the British Museum (Harleian MS. 4425); and the copies were probably painted by Edmund Thomas Parris (1793–1873).

To another art historian I owe a further example of a painter's introduction of a manuscript into his composition. Professor Francis Haskell told me of the charming portrait of Victor Hugo's daughter, Léopoldine (1824–43), drowned with her husband six months after her marriage. The picture, *Léopoldine au Livre d'Heures*, by Auguste de Châtillon (Frontispiece), was painted in August 1835, when the girl was eleven. Monsieur Pierre Georgel, in whose book the portrait is reproduced,[1] comments upon the accuracy of the artist's depiction of the girl's dress and the armchair after known originals, and doubtless the Book of Hours, with its miniature of the death of the Virgin, is an exact copy also.

Quel beau missel gothique
Enrichi par vos mains d'un dessin fantastique?

asks Victor Hugo in a poem written two years later; and the identification of the manuscript would not be beyond the bounds of possibility. And has artistic licence enlarged and elongated the book? This is one's first impression, and then doubts are sown by the recollection of those long thin Books of Hours executed for members of the Talbot family, two of which are in the Fitzwilliam Museum at Cambridge.

On a more learned plane the works of John Obadiah Westwood (1805–93) were significant. This remarkable self-taught palaeographer and entomologist devoted his exiguous private means to the pursuit of learning, and became the leading authority on Anglo-Saxon and medieval manuscripts, as well as a distinguished entomologist. Most of his books lie outside our period, but not *Palaeographia Sacra Pictoria*, 1843–5, a work which set a new standard for the quality and fidelity of its plates. Westwood's Introduction contains a useful survey of the previous authorities on palaeography

[1] *Léopoldine; une jeune fille romantique*, Paris, 1967, from which my information is derived. I am much indebted to M. Georgel, to Professor J. B. Barrère, and to Mademoiselle Martine Écalle, curator of the Maison de Victor Hugo, where the portrait hangs today.

and allied subjects. His own merit lies especially in his pioneering the establishment of certain national schools of illumination. In some respects his claims to priority are perhaps too highly pitched. He had 'clearly established', he asserted, 'the fact of an existence of a native school of religion and art on our sister island [Ireland] by a series of facsimiles from Irish manuscripts, executed between the 7th and 10th centuries, although the existence of such documents had been denied, not only by Astle and other palaeographers, but also by the latest Irish historians', a statement which seems to do less than justice to the researches of O'Conor, Madden, and Sir William Betham.[1] His aim, he said, was to be the first to present palaeography, calligraphy, illumination, and miniature painting as one homogeneous theme. He insists on the superiority of Irish and Anglo-Saxon book-decoration over all contemporary schools, and sharply takes issue with Ottley, whom he alleges to have asserted that 'nothing is more fallacious than the idea of being able to determine the ages of MSS. and ancient inscriptions from the particular forms of their characters, and the existence of various national styles of writing is a mere fanciful suggestion'. This, however, seems to me to misrepresent Ottley's views, or rather to make him appear to have asserted generally what was in fact a piece of very special pleading in his *Archaeologia* article on the Aratus in the British Museum (Harleian MS. 647),[2] in which Ottley was mistakenly attempting the impossible task of proving that a manuscript written in a Carolingian minuscule was really of the second or third century in date. Westwood in fact displays the quality often to be observed in autodidacts, a tendency to denigrate other workers in the field. He was one of the last writers to regard the art of illumination as a steady chronological progression towards excellence. In his account of Sir John Soane's Clovio manuscript he traces the course of Italian illumination from the thirteenth century onwards, and ends: 'Nothing can, in fact, exceed the difference between the works of this artist Clovio and those of his fellow-countrymen two hundred years before his time. Theirs—for

[1] *Irish Antiquarian Researches*, i, Dublin, 1827, contains long accounts of The Book of Dimma and The Book of Armagh.

[2] *Archaeologia*, xxvi (1836), pp. 47–214.

the most part stiff and heavy, with all the characteristics of the worst period of the Byzantine School—and his, among the most marvellous copies of nature, perhaps, ever executed.'

No British works, however, can vie in splendour with two noble French productions, the first Silvestre and Champollion's well-known *Paléographie Universelle*, published in four great folio volumes in 1841, and, as its title suggests, ranging far more widely than the subject of this book, although many fine miniatures are incidentally reproduced therein. Madden edited an English translation of this work in 1850.[1] The second is the superb unfinished life-work of that dedicated student of illuminated manuscripts the Comte Auguste de Bastard d'Estang (1792–1883). His *Peintures et Ornements des Manuscrits* was one of those works, planned on such universal and perfectionist lines that even with generous Government assistance it was inconceivable that it would be completed on the scale on which it was begun. In the event, twenty parts only were published, each of eight plates, from 1835 onwards. Even in its truncated form it represents perhaps the grandest series of coloured facsimiles of manuscripts ever published. Its very high cost, its extreme rarity, and the absence of explanatory text, rendered it hardly influential in our period; indeed Westwood, in his Introduction to *Palaeographia Sacra Pictoria*, doubted whether there were more than two copies in England. The Comte de Bastard's extensive materials for the work passed to the Bibliothèque Nationale, and were the subject of an elaborate catalogue by Léopold Delisle.[2] Their value was enhanced by the fact that the Comte recorded certain manuscripts which no longer survive, the famous twelfth-century *Hortus Deliciarum*, for example, which perished at Strasbourg in 1870.

The Comte de Bastard, however, has another special claim to our notice as the first critic to recognize and assert the supreme quality of the miniatures of Jean Foucquet. In 1834 he conceived the plan of reproducing in colour all the miniatures in the first volume of the Josephus, and then extended his design to cover the whole of the

[1] *Silvestre's Universal Paleography, the Historical and Descriptive Letter-Press by Champollion-Figeac, and Champollion Jr.*, trans. into English, with considerable additional corrections, by Sir F. Madden, 2 vols., 1850.

[2] L. V. Delisle: *Les Collections de Bastard d'Estang*, Paris, 1885.

Master of Tours's *œuvre.*[1] In 1838 he wrote that Foucquet was 'a worthy precursor of Leonardo da Vinci, Albrecht Durer, Holbein and Raphael', and that 'he took a flight so lofty that he should be granted a place among these great masters and in future be named with them'. These are strong words: I cannot recall even Clovio being ranked with Leonardo. Volume II of the Josephus, as we have seen, lurked at this date unrecognized in England, and indeed about this time was probably divested of all but one of its miniatures. In 1833 the art historian J. D. Passavant had recognized one of the dismembered Foucquet miniatures from the Hours of Étienne Chevalier in the collection of Samuel Rogers.[2] I should like to know the circumstances under which that famous manuscript was cut up early in the eighteenth century, long before the vogue for collecting single miniatures made such acts of vandalism common.

In the years 1830–50 many new collectors of illuminated manuscripts emerged. Moreover, this was the period in which the collectors of Old Masters began in greatly increasing numbers to add as a matter of course to their cabinets and galleries the picture-books of the Middle Ages. Striking evidence of this is to be found in the membership of the Burlington Club, founded for art-collectors in 1856. In spite of the existence of the Roxburghe Club and the Philobiblon Society to cater for their special interests, it is remarkable how many collectors whom we think of primarily as collectors of manuscripts are to be found in the Burlington Club's list—Robert Curzon and Walter Sneyd, the Duke of Hamilton, R. S. Holford, and John Ruskin. There were also several members whom we recognize among collectors of printed books, such as Frederick Locker, William Stirling of Keir, and the sociable and cultured Belgian Minister in London, Baron Sylvain van de Weyer: and those who joined within a few years included such well-known owners of manuscripts as the Baroness Burdett Coutts, the Duc d'Aumale, and John Malcolm of Poltalloch. From sale catalogues, from the works

[1] See Paul Durrieu, *Les Antiquités judaïques et le peintre Jean Foucquet*, Paris, 1908.

[2] J. D. Passavant, *Tour of a German Artist in England*, i, 1836, pp. 194–5. Samuel Rogers's small but choice group of manuscripts and single miniatures were sold with his pictures by Christie on 28 Apr. to 10 May 1856. An album of miniatures formed by him is B.M. Add. MS. 21412.

of Dr. Waagen, who went out of his way to record collections of illuminated manuscripts, and from a score of other sources, a formidable body of evidence can be amassed about the collectors of the nineteenth century; and rather than indulge in a breathless bout of name-dropping it seemed wiser to study a few collections in some detail.

Foremost among these the reader would expect to find the splendid series of manuscripts gathered together by the Marquess of Douglas, later the 10th Duke of Hamilton (1767–1852).[1] Many of them had indeed been bought at a slightly earlier period than that covered by this chapter, for he already owned an important collection by 1819, when it was described in William Clarke's *Repertorium Bibliographicum* in an account which was supplied by the Duke's father-in-law, William Beckford. It would have been agreeable to follow the career of the Duke, who dressed to the last 'in a military laced undress coat, tights and Hessian boots', to his final resting place in the Egyptian sarcophagus housed in the great mausoleum he built at Hamilton Palace; and it would have been instructive to record the dispersal of his art collections for little short of £400,000. But Beckford's son-in-law, and the inheritor of his library, is Mr. Hobson's province, and we must eagerly await a fuller treatment of this great connoisseur than could be fitted into the framework of this book. Instead, I propose to treat of a collector with an eye for quality and the means to indulge it without stint, Robert Stayner Holford (1808–92).

If one wished to depict an Ideal Connoisseur the result might well resemble Robert Holford. With his long hair, imperial beard, wide-brimmed black hat, and much be-frogged cloak he looked more like a spruce Dante Gabriel Rossetti than a millionaire who changed the appearance of central London by erecting in Park Lane his vast Italianate palace, Dorchester House. He was the son of George Peter Holford, of Westonbirt in Gloucestershire, and was educated at Harrow and Oriel College, Oxford, where he took his B.A. in 1829.

[1] See Helmut Boese, *Die Lateinischen Handschriften der Sammlung Hamilton zu Berlin*, fol., Wiesbaden, 1966, the Introduction of which, pp. ix–xxv, gives the fullest account available of Hamilton as a collector of manuscripts.

There was a brief flirtation with the Law—he was entered a student of Lincoln's Inn on 6 November 1828—but he had no need to earn his living, for he was an only child, and the fortunes of his family were based, in the words of his son-in-law, on 'hereditary thrift, along with a *cache* of bullion buried on the estate of an uncle in the Isle of Wight during the threat of Napoleonic invasion'.

Holford was a collector of catholic tastes. His pictures ranged from the Evangelist miniatures of a ninth-century Gospels to a portrait of Castlereagh by Lawrence. His collection of prints, especially his matchless series of Rembrandt etchings, fetched over £28,000 at auction in 1893. His printed books were greatly enriched by the purchase, about 1840, of a large part of the library of the fifth Lord Vernon (1803–66), the authority on Dante. When Dr. Waagen visited him, Dorchester House was being built, and the collections were examined at the house in Russell Square formerly occupied by Sir Thomas Lawrence. Waagen commended Holford's taste and judgement highly, especially in regard to the manuscripts with miniatures, 'as attractive in my eyes', he said, 'as any other department of his works of art, and . . . as valuable as any to be found in public museums'; and he particularly remarked on Holford's civility in allowing him to examine the manuscripts alone and at leisure, 'a kindness', he added, 'which I mention as contrasting favourably with the habits of other owners of MSS. in England'. As a result he was able to devote seventeen pages to a description of eighteen of the finest manuscripts.[1] Two illustrated catalogues,[2] however, published in the present century, give us a fuller picture of their range and quality.

By one of the curiosities of connoisseurship it happens that almost every Holford manuscript of the first quality is now in the United States. They were on the market in the late 1920s, when the great Dr. Rosenbach was at the height of his powers, before any form of export control had been introduced, and at a time when the great private American buyers were striving to redress, in a few decades,

[1] *Treasures of Art in Great Britain*, ii, 1854, pp. 205–22.

[2] Sir George Lindsay Holford: *The Holford Collection*, London, 1924; and *The Holford Collection, Dorchester House*, 2 vols., Oxford, 1927.

the balance hitherto in favour of the libraries of the old world, achieved over centuries.

Pride of place must go to the Gospels, written in letters of gold at Rheims in the ninth century, and now Pierpont Morgan Library MS. 728. This, in common with most of his finest things, had been acquired by Holford from Payne and Foss. They were also the source of Morgan MS. 736, the twelfth-century Miracles of St. Edmund, with thirty-two large miniatures, which had cost Holford £300 in 1841. In the Morgan Library are also two splendid thirteenth-century books from Holford's collection, No. 729, the Amiens Psalter and Hours, with forty miniatures, which, as we saw in a previous chapter (p. 68), Ottley dismembered and Dr. Millar finally reconstructed; and No. 730, another Psalter and Hours, probably Cambrai, with thirty-one miniatures. Holford had bought this book through Rodd, at the sale of Benjamin Heywood Bright on 18 June 1844, at which it was illustrated as the frontispiece of the catalogue and fetched £225, a substantial sum for a thirteenth-century book at that date, and a sign of the changing values in the market for Gothic art.

Holford had another book written at the turn of the same century, of the very first rank. In the New York Public Library is the wonderful *Bible Historiée*,[1] bought from Payne and Foss in 1837, a book with more than a thousand miniatures, which was a source of wonder and delight to William Morris and Edward Burne-Jones. The latter, indeed, claimed that 'if a new flood came and submerged the earth, this book saved would serve to regenerate Art'. Holford owned several first-class manuscripts of the fifteenth and sixteenth centuries, and here it must suffice to mention Morgan MS. 732, a Book of Hours adorned with eight large miniatures by Jean Bourdichon of Tours.

The sixty or more single miniatures which were such a feature of the Holford Collection were mainly derived from Ottley's sale of 1838, and were mostly of course from Choir Books of the fifteenth and early sixteenth centuries. Holford, however, also bought earlier leaves, such as the twelfth-century examples from a Bury St.

[1] Spencer MS. 22.

Edmunds Psalter, painted with twenty-five scenes.[1] Four leaves only of this wonderful book survive, and if Ottley dismembered it, it is difficult to forgive him.

Holford, with his great houses in Park Lane and at Westonbirt, his *arboretum* and art-collections, his passionate concern for detail and design, which led him to employ Alfred Stevens for eighteen years, deserves more extended study than he has yet received. For us he must typify the earliest of the great British collectors who recognized that in the formation of a collection of pictures the inclusion of book-painting along with easel-painting was essential.

Early in May 1836 the British Museum acquired one of its greatest treasures, the Alcuin Bible,[2] written about 840 and decorated with four full-page miniatures (Plate 16). Immediately after the completion of the purchase Madden published a long account of the manuscript and others of the same group in *The Gentleman's Magazine*.[3] Madden's article was remarkable, in that it contained a severe attack on the good faith and veracity of the vendor. The circumstances under which this famous book was hawked (the word is not too strong) round the libraries of Europe throw some light on the market in manuscripts at this period, and are, I hope, worth recounting in some detail.

The seller was Monsieur J. H. de Speyr Passavant of Basle. I have so far discovered very little about him.[4] Both the von Speyr and the Passavant families were prominent as bankers in Basle in the early nineteenth century. On the title-page of a catalogue of his collection, printed at Basle in 1835, he describes himself as J. H. de Speyr, *l'aîné*, and his Basle address is given as Heuberg No. 415. This catalogue contains, as well as the Alcuin Bible, other manuscripts, a group of ancient and modern medals, 3,000 books, some stained glass, armour, tapestries, and a collection of pictures which bear resounding names, seven, for example, Dürer's.

The early history of the Alcuin Bible is obscure. In the early seventeenth century it was the property of the monastery of Moûtier-

[1] Pierpont Morgan MS. 521.

[2] Add. MS. 10546.

[3] *Gentleman's Magazine*, N.S. vi (1836), pp. 358–63, 468–77, 580–7: for this account I have also drawn upon his journal.

[4] The B.M. catalogue gives his real name as Pierre Julien Fontaine.

Grand-Val, near Basle; and at the sequestration of that house's possessions under French occupation in 1793 it was bought by M. Bennot, Vice-President of the Tribunal of Delémont, from whom de Speyr, as we will call him, bought the manuscript in 1822.

Even at that date it was, by any standards, a noble possession: but de Speyr, whom I take to have been a dealer, set to work to demonstrate that it was nobler still. He sought to prove that it was written in the hand of Alcuin himself and completed in 800, that it was handed to Charlemagne at his coronation on 1 January 801, and that it featured in Charlemagne's will in 811. Once this was established, de Speyr argued, French national pride would find its acquisition irresistible, even at the most extravagant of prices.

Accordingly, in December 1828 he took the manuscript to Paris, encouraged by the Chevalier d'Horrer, French Chargé d'Affaires in Switzerland. In Paris he called on every librarian, bookseller, and savant, and from many of them extracted certificates of commendation, some of which took at face value the owner's opinion of his book. Some indeed were cautious. Champollion, for example, merely described it as 'one of the most beautiful and most ancient of its kind', whereas Van Praet referred to it unequivocally as 'the Bible presented by Alcuin to Charlemagne'. Cumulatively, these high appraisals from every authority were impressive—the De Bure brothers, Renouard, Firmin Didot, Nodier, Peignot, Brunet, archivists, bishops, historians; de Speyr had shown remarkable industry in the collection of testimonials, and many of them underlined the real purpose of his visit. 'It is difficult to believe', wrote Guizot, 'that this wonderful manuscript, once it has entered France, should ever leave it', and he exhorted the Government to take action to prevent it.

These certificates were printed by de Speyr in a pamphlet published in Paris in October 1829,[1] along with a historical and palaeographical account of the manuscript, a compilation which contained, wrote Madden sourly,

> so many *false* statements and displays such a mixture of *ignorance* and *charlatanerie*, concealed under an assumed veil of criticism and learning,

[1] *Description de la Bible écrite par Alcuin*, Paris, 1829.

as to render some more impartial account absolutely necessary—more especially since many individuals in France, distinguished for their bibliographical attainments, have been induced by the hardihood of Mr. de Speyr Passavant's assertions to sacrifice their opinions to his, or to add weight to such assertions by yielding credence to them, and repeating them.

Madden's statement is, to say the least, disingenuous, for, as we shall see, he had himself shown the compliance on which he remarks in his French counterparts.

In Paris de Speyr circulated his pamphlet, accompanied by petitions, addresses, and letters, to the King, his ministers, and the officers of the Bibliothèque du Roi, urging the purchase upon them. His opening price was 60,000 francs, a figure lowered by successive stages to 48,000 and then 42,000. But a price which seemed excessive, coupled with an incessant sales campaign, defeated its ends: the French Government refused to treat for the manuscript.

The owner was not unduly discouraged, for before 30 April 1829 he had already offered it to Lord Stuart de Rothesay, British Ambassador in Paris, and in December of the same year to the greatest of English collectors of Bibles, the Duke of Sussex. But the price was the stumbling-block. In October 1834, so Madden informs us, the vendor 'despatched letters to the Archbishops both of Canterbury and of York, the Duke of Sussex (again), and "the right laudable Lord Viscount Althorp" in England; to Baron Reiffenberg in Belgium; and to the Bishop of Beauvais in France, offering his MS. to each, and protesting he had given him or his country the preference!' No sale resulted, but England obviously seemed a more promising area of operation, and in January 1836 the indefatigable de Speyr set out on a visit, bearing his manuscript with him.

Here the French pattern was repeated. Testimonials were solicited and received. The Duke of Hamilton, who was doubtless approached as a potential purchaser, hoped that the book might find its home in London alongside the most beautiful relics of Athens and of Rome. At Oxford Doctors Bandinel and Bliss, and at the British Museum the Revd. Josiah Forshall, secretary to the Trustees, authenticated its antiquity, but were cautious about endorsing de Speyr's higher claims. Sir Frederic Madden, however, was less critical. 'I have seen and examined', he wrote, 'with great care and equal satisfaction the magnificent MS. Bible belonging to Mr. de Speyr Passavant, and I am of opinion, that it is unquestionably the volume written for Charlemagne by Alcuin, and of the highest value and interest.'

It seems a little odd that two officers of the British Museum should have contributed testimonials designed to raise the book's price, at a time when negotiations were in train between the owner and the Museum. The impossibly high figure, however, which de Speyr set on his possession may well have made any sale seem a very remote prospect. £12,000 was the first sum proposed, then £8,000, and finally, 'as an immense sacrifice', £6,500. Eventually de Speyr, discovering that no English collector or librarian would contemplate bargaining with him on the basis of such figures as these, decided to consign his manuscript to the auction room: and, together with another manuscript, a few printed books, some paintings, a small altar, and an ancient poignard, the Alcuin Bible was offered for sale, by Evans of Pall Mall, on 27 April 1836.

The description of the manuscript (lot 9) filled six pages, and the cataloguer exhausted his stock of superlatives in the process. Accompanying the lot was an album in which the testimonials of the distinguished *literati* had been bound, and the most eloquent of them, including Madden's, were printed in the catalogue. A resounding peroration exhorted 'some spirited individual, or a Public Library' to secure 'this Inestimable Treasure'.

Inestimable it may have seemed, but greatly to the credit of the Museum authorities some hard estimating had been conducted by the officers and the Trustees. It must have been sorely tempting to wash their hands of the whole affair, but an opportunity such as this demanded and received extraordinary exertions; and in the event Forshall attended the sale with authority to bid up to the very substantial sum of 600 guineas. One cannot help wondering whether the vendor had got wind of this figure, because the bidding was opened by the auctioneer at £700. Thereafter, Madden recorded in his journal, there was not a single *bona fide* advance: but the auctioneer, in the mysterious manner of the profession, contrived, by picking imaginary bids off the ceiling, to run the price up to £1,500, at which it was bought in for the vendor.

'The result having brought M. de Speyr Passavant in some measure to his senses,' wrote Madden in *The Gentleman's Magazine*, 'overtures were made to him on the part of the Trustees of the Museum, and the Manuscript finally became the property of the nation for the (comparatively) moderate sum of 750£.' It would seem that the main initiative came from Forshall, for in his journal on 28 April Madden recorded that he had declined 'at present' Forshall's request that he should write a letter setting out the book's value, which Forshall could lay before the Trustees. On 4 May, however, both men were at work on the subject, looking up information on the other Bibles associated with Alcuin. On this occasion Forshall told Madden that there seemed to him to have been suspicious alterations on the penultimate leaf, and that in particular the crucial word CAROLUS had been tampered with. Madden, vexed that he had not seen this himself, drove hastily down to Evans's rooms again for a further inspection, and conceded that indeed CAROLUS and other words had been rewritten or retouched in recent times. This discovery was in fact something of a red herring, and it is generally accepted that the retouching represents innocent replacement of words and letters accidentally damaged by some adhesive substance. But since de Speyr's claims for the book rested heavily on the line of verse

Is Carolus qui jam scribere jussit eum,

it was natural that apprehensions should have been aroused.

Madden's long article in *The Gentleman's Magazine*, in which he draws parallels with nine other coeval Bibles in Continental libraries, had, I believe, a variety of motives. He was concerned to announce to the learned world that the British Museum had acquired this splendid manuscript, and had succeeded, in contrast with the French, in negotiating its purchase at a realistic figure, instead of the ludicrous sum which the owner had originally put upon it. It was also his aim to set out soberly the very great value and interest of the manuscript, belief in which had been undermined by de Speyr's campaign of high-pressure salesmanship; and in this context he sought to correct the extravagant claims made in the vendor's pamphlet, the assertion, for example, that this very book had been mentioned in Charlemagne's will. And, finally, there would have been a natural desire to set his own record straight and beat a tactical retreat from his perhaps over-enthusiastic endorsement of the book's merits, which must have been the source of some vexation when he saw them used for advertising purposes in the sale catalogue.

At the end of our period a new figure appears and turns a critical eye on the subject of this study—the professional art historian. Dr. Gustav Waagen (1744–1868), Director of the Royal Gallery in Berlin, spent five months in England in 1835 and a further eight months in 1850 and 1851. The books these tours produced, *Works of Art and Artists in England*, 3 vols., 1838, and *Treasures of Art in Great Britain*, 3 vols., 1854, with a Supplement, 1857, are still part of the standard equipment of art historians today. With tireless industry Waagen located and described thousands of pictures in British collections, both public and private. He represents the archetypal Teutonic Kunstforscher, whom, until the 1930s (and some might say later still) most Englishmen regarded with high respect, not unmixed with amused condescension. He was, in fact, something of a figure of fun, as he shortsightedly peered at pictures in the intervals of concerts, and interlarded his publications with judgements, mostly flattering, on English girls, beds, roast beef, and plum pudding. His misadventures in stately homes would make an essay in themselves—the floors, for example, were up at Windsor, owing to the installation of central heating; and at Woburn the housekeeper refused to draw the curtains and hurried him through darkened rooms. Even when his host was all attentiveness, there could be disadvantages. At Hamilton Palace Waagen reported that he 'enjoyed the favour of having the most costly manuscripts shown to me by the Duke himself, the Duchess being also present and evincing a lively interest. My sensations however were of rather a mixed nature . . . For, no sooner did I pause to consider some of the more beautiful miniatures more closely, than the Duke remarked, that it would take weeks to study them at that rate, and urged me on. This being the case, it was utterly impossible for me to make a single memorandum.' In general, however, this passionate Anglophile evoked affection in his English friends. 'Dr Waagen', wrote Lady Eastlake in her journal, 'is a most intelligent, clever, witty old gentleman, full of mimicry and drollery, and more well-bred than most Germans—but he was educated at Hamburg, and says he imbibed many English habits. He speaks English very imperfectly, but is inventive and original.'[1]

Wilhelm Waetzoldt, in his *Deutsche Kunsthistoriker*,[2] points out that Waagen brought to art the new critical methods by which Niebuhr had revolutionized the writing of history, and showed 'a new eye for style, composition, colour and form'. His recognition of miniatures as part of the history of art dated back as early as 1818, when he had examined manuscripts in Heidelberg University Library. Seroux d'Agincourt had, of course, shown a lively interest in them, but Waagen, as Waetzoldt emphasizes, was the first man to give them their proper importance. He projected a history of medieval miniature painting, which he never lived to publish, and from the study of miniatures Waagen hoped, in his own words, 'to illuminate the total night of the Arts, from which Johann Van Eyck suddenly emerged as a star of the first rank'.

Here is Waagen's justification of his new standpoint, from the first edition of his guide to English collections:

Another branch of the fine arts of which the English are very fond, were Mss. illustrated with miniatures, which are of so much importance in the history of painting; for, as greater monuments of the early centuries of the middle ages are entirely wanting in most countries in Europe, and are very rare in others, it is only by means of those miniatures that we can obtain knowledge of the state of painting from the fourth to the fifteenth century. They teach us how Christian art, long faithful to its mother the antique, in the conception and mechanical part, gradually assumed in both a new and peculiar manner, and how, subsequently, the ideas of the different nations were impressed upon it . . . From them proceeded even the whole of the great advance of the art of painting, both in Italy and the Netherlands in the fifteenth century. For the celebrated Fiesole, who was the first in Italy who in his paintings made the happiest use of the variety

[1] *Journals and Correspondence*, ed. C. Eastlake Smith, i, 1895, p. 249.

[2] 2nd edn., ii, Berlin, 1965, pp. 29–45.

of intellectual expression in the human countenance, and thereby led to a new era in the arts, was the pupil of a miniature painter, and first cultivated that property in this branch of the art. In like manner, the celebrated brothers, Hubert and John Van Eyck, the founder of the great Flemish school, were essentially disciples of that great school of miniature painters, which in the second half of the fourteenth century was so flourishing, and had attained so high a degree of perfection in the Netherlands . . .[1]

This theme he developed in his *Treasures of Art*, but his most important manifesto on the subject was obscurely printed in the first volume of the *Bibliographical and Historical Miscellanies* of the Philobiblon Society, distributed to its members in 1854. One hundred copies only were printed, and this may account for the fact that I have never seen this paper cited or quoted. Nevertheless, Waagen's nine-page essay, 'On the Importance of Manuscripts with Miniatures in the History of Art', seems to be one of those key documents in the history of palaeography and art criticism which would well deserve re-publication if ever a collection of such things were brought together.

In the four volumes of his second work Waagen described over 250 manuscripts with miniatures, a total that enormously exceeded any previous work in this field. The public collections in which groups of manuscripts are singled out for description are mainly those one would expect—the British Museum, the Bodleian, and Cambridge University Library; the Soane Museum, the Hunterian Collection at Glasgow, and Durham Cathedral Library. In the private sphere he published notes on a number of manuscripts at Hamilton Palace, Holkham, and Chatsworth, as well as on those in the collections of the Duc d'Aumale (now at Chantilly), of Robert Holford, and of an interesting and today a little-known collector, the Oxford astronomer, Manuel John Johnson (1805–59).[2] Indeed not the least valuable parts of Waagen's books are the descriptions of visits, or the references to collectors about whom information is otherwise hard to find. How many scholars today, I wonder, can recall anything about the manuscripts of the Revd. John Fuller

1 *Works of Art and Artists in England*, i, 1838, pp. 59–60.

2 *Treasures of Art*, iii, 1854, pp. 112–20: Johnson's books and manuscripts were sold at Sotheby's in a sale beginning on 27 May 1862.

Russell,[1] of Eagle House, near Enfield? Waagen's book is indeed full of clues, one of which was followed up thanks to a lead from Sir Roger Mynors, who told me that Lord Clark possessed an album of medieval miniatures, put together by the Scottish antiquary James Dennistoun (1803–55), author of *Memoirs of the Dukes of Urbino*, 1851.[2] Dennistoun toured the Continent collecting pictures and antiques in 1825 and 1826, and in 1836 he went to Italy, where he lived for twelve years. Waagen gives a brief account of some of his pictures,[3] and his connoisseurship is highly rated (he was the first man to identify Piero della Francesca). The notes attached to Lord Clark's album, which originally contained 105 miniatures, show Dennistoun to have had a good eye. Dates of acquisition reveal the collector acquiring miniatures at Munich in 1836, at Florence in 1837, at Gubbio and Lucca in 1838, and at Padua in 1839, and he records that a French miniature of the fourteenth century, 'the long contorted figures of which afford a perfect specimen of the French style', was given to him by the Abbé Celotti in 1838. His dating of the handful of Greek miniatures with which the volume starts is optimistically early, but thereafter the Italian schools of illumination are differentiated with an acuteness very rare in the 1830s. Ottley apart, it is difficult to name a connoisseur of this date prepared to label miniatures as 'Lombardo-Venetian' or 'passing from the manner of Beato Angelico into that introduced by Domenico Ghirlandaio'. Dennistoun is said to have collected materials for a history of religious painting, but to have passed them to his friend Lord Lindsay for incorporation in the latter's *Sketches of the History of Christian Art*.

Large sections of Waagen are readable for the *personalia* they contain. We can hear Ottley's voice, full of pleased surprise, when he exclaimed that ever since he had returned to England from Italy no one had paid so much attention to his Italian primitives as Waagen: and when, after dinner, Waagen leafed through Ottley's portfolios, containing 1,000 miniatures cut out of old vellum manuscripts, we can imagine him concealing from his host the vexation, afterwards

[1] *Treasures of Art*, ii, 1854, pp. 461–4; sales at Sotheby's on 26 June 1885 and 1 Feb. 1886.

[2] A memoir of Dennistoun is prefixed to Edward Hutton's edition of *The Dukes of Urbino*, 3 vols., 1909. He also reprints the catalogue of the sale of his pictures, held by Christie on 14 June 1855.

[3] *Treasures of Art*, iii, 1854, pp. 281–2.

expressed in print, because 'the miniatures being thus detached from the documents to which they originally belonged, they are unfortunately deprived of the principal means of ascertaining the place and time of their origin'. We can sympathize with his frustrations at the British Museum in 1835, when he was only permitted to inspect a few manuscripts, the reference numbers of which he had 'with infinite trouble found elsewhere', and rejoice with him that in 1850 a new era had dawned and that 'by the kindness of Sir Frederic Madden and Mr Holmes' he was 'allowed the freest access to all the treasures under their care'.

With many of Waagen's judgements we cannot today concur; for pioneer art historians had greater opportunities of giving hostages to fortune than their successors. Occasionally Dr. Waagen confessed to fallibility and took refuge in vagueness. 'The decorations of the borders', he remarked of one of Manuel Johnson's manuscripts, 'show a mixture of German, Netherlandish and Italian varieties of taste'; but there are attributions to, or parallels with, Giotto, Rogier van der Weyden, Hans Memling, or the Van Eycks. The hands of the last, indeed, Waagen was wont to see in many unexpected places, and later art historians have suggested that his eye was less than first-class. It is a little disconcerting, for example, to find in his description of MS. Douce 29 a discussion whether the date on folio 356 is 1510 or 1540, when in fact Waagen had before him the word *isto* in capitals—though, I suppose, this might happen to any of us on an off-day. But these are pin-pricks: Waagen was a giant, and with his appearance the study of medieval miniatures assumed the form in which we know it today. I believe, however, that his great book has been less studied by those concerned with manuscripts than it deserves; and this belief was given striking support when I was working in the Bodleian. His four volumes had been well thumbed by the historians of pictures, but, in a library where manuscripts are not neglected, I was the first man in over a century to take a paper-knife to some of the sections which described the manuscript treasures of the British Museum.

It was, of course, John Ruskin who was the popular mouthpiece of the new appreciation of thirteenth-century art, just outside the terminal date we have set ourselves: for Ruskin did not start expounding his views on medieval manuscripts until the 1850s. These views were, to say the least, idiosyncratic, but none the less influential for that. He has described the almost mystical impact made on him by his first purchase of a little fourteenth-century Book of Hours. 'Truly', he wrote, 'a well-illuminated missal is a fairy cathedral full of painted windows, bound together to carry in one's pocket, with the music and the blessing of all its prayers besides.'[1] Ruskin lacked all liturgical knowledge and had no feeling for an illuminated manuscript as a whole. Hence arose the cheerful dismemberment from the highest motives. 'Cut missal up in evening—hard work', ran a diary entry in 1854; and there are more deliberate testaments to this cause. 'There are literally thousands of manuscripts in the libraries of England . . . of which a few leaves, dispersed among parish schools, would do more to educate the children of the poor than all the catechisms that ever tortured them.' Hence those bits of books at St. George's Guild and Cheltenham Ladies College, and those exhortations to the public to patronize illuminators and to provide themselves with heirlooms for posterity. 'Dr Waagen,' wrote Ruskin, 'of such mighty name as a Connoisseur, was a most double-dyed ass'; nevertheless, he drew upon his works heavily—'an intolerable fool—a good authority only in matters of tradition', he complained, as he made pages of notes.[2]

Ruskin's originality lay in proclaiming for the first time that the greatest period of illumination was the century between 1250 and 1350. For him this period, still denigrated by older connoisseurs, represented the culmination of the illuminator's art. After 1350 there was a falling away, and the standards dropped, Ruskin asserted, until the time of Giulio Clovio, when they reached the lowest level of all. And on that pronouncement, based on standards diametrically opposed to those we have been studying over the previous century, we have traced the full transition brought about by the Gothic Revival in a limited area of connoisseurship.

[1] *Praeterita*, iii: *Works*, ed. Cook and Wedderburn, xxxv, 1908, pp. 490–1.

[2] For Ruskin's manuscripts see Mr. James S. Dearden's excellent article, 'John Ruskin, the Collector', *The Library*, 5th Ser. xxi. 2 (June 1966), pp. 124–54.

Index of Manuscripts

General Index

There is a separate index of the illuminated manuscripts cited, arranged by present locations. The general index also contains a selected group of famous manuscripts, e.g. Alcuin Bible.